PRENTICE-HALL FOUNDATIONS OF PHILOSOPHY SERIES

03.95

Virgil Aldrich	PHILOSOPHY OF ART
William Alston	PHILOSOPHY OF LANGUAGE
Stephen Barker	PHILOSOPHY OF MATHEMATICS
Roderick Chisholm	THEORY OF KNOWLEDGE
William Dray	PHILOSOPHY OF HISTORY
William Frankena	ETHICS
Carl Hempel	PHILOSOPHY OF NATURAL SCIENCE
John Hick	PHILOSOPHY OF RELIGION
Sidney Hook	POLITICAL PHILOSOPHY
John Lenz	PHILOSOPHY OF EDUCATION
Richard Rudner	PHILOSOPHY OF SOCIAL SCIENCE
Wesley Salmon	LOGIC
Richard Taylor	METAPHYSICS

Elizabeth and Monroe Beardsley, editors

Philosophy of History

PHILOSOPHY

OF HISTORY

FOUNDATIONS OF PHILOSOPHY SERIES

William H. Dray

University of Toronto

PRENTICE-HALL, INC.   ENGLEWOOD CLIFFS, N. J.

PHILOSOPHY OF HISTORY, Dray

FOUNDATIONS OF PHILOSOPHY SERIES

C-66384

PRENTICE-HALL INTERNATIONAL, INC., London

PRENTICE-HALL OF AUSTRALIA, PTY., LTD., Sydney

PRENTICE-HALL OF CANADA, LTD., Toronto

PRENTICE-HALL OF INDIA (PRIVATE) LTD., New Delhi

PRENTICE-HALL OF JAPAN, INC., Tokyo

Current printing (last digit):

11   10

FOUNDATIONS

OF PHILOSOPHY

Many of the problems of philosophy are of such broad relevance to human concerns, and so complex in their ramifications, that they are, in one form or another, perennially present. Though in the course of time they yield in part to philosophical inquiry, they may need to be rethought by each age in the light of its broader scientific knowledge and deepened ethical and religious experience. Better solutions are found by more refined and rigorous methods. Thus, one who approaches the study of philosophy in the hope of understanding the best of what it affords will look for both fundamental issues and contemporary achievements.

Written by a group of distinguished philosophers, the Foundations of Philosophy Series aims to exhibit some of the main problems in the various fields of philosophy as they stand at the present stage of philosophical history.

While certain fields are likely to be represented in most introductory courses in philosophy, college classes differ widely in emphasis, in method of instruction, and in rate of progress. Every instructor needs freedom to change his course as his own philosophical interests, the size and makeup of his classes, and the needs of his students vary from year to year. The thirteen volumes in the Foundations of Philosophy Series—each complete in itself, but complementing the others—offer a new flexibility to the instructor, who can create his own textbook by combining several volumes as he wishes, and can choose different combinations at different times. Those volumes that are not used in an introductory course will be found valuable, along with other texts or collections of readings, for the more specialized upper-level courses.

ELIZABETH BEARDSLEY   MONROE BEARDSLEY

ACKNOWLEDGMENTS

A large part of Chapter 3 of this book is adapted from "The Historian's Problem of Selection," originally published in *Logic, Methodology and Philosophy of Science*, edited by Ernest Nagel, Patrick Suppes, and Alfred Tarski. Chapter 4 incorporates, with slight changes, "Some Causal Accounts of the American Civil War," originally published in the Summer 1962 issue of *Daedalus*. I am grateful to the Stanford University Press and to the American Academy of Arts and Sciences for their generous permission to use this material in its present form.

WILLIAM H. DRAY

CONTENTS

Philosophy of History

CRITICAL AND SPECULATIVE

An introduction to philosophy of history must begin by distinguishing two senses which the word "history" commonly bears. On the one hand, we use it to refer to the course of events: a certain stratum of reality, which historians make it their professional business to study. On the other, we use it to denote the historian's study itself: we mean by it a certain kind of inquiry into a certain kind of subject matter. Corresponding to these senses are philosophical disciplines, often referred to as speculative and critical philosophy of history.[1] The speculative seeks to discover in history, the course of events, a pattern or meaning which lies beyond the purview of the ordinary historian. The critical endeavors to make clear the nature of the historian's own inquiry, in order to "locate" it, as it were, on the map of knowledge. This book cannot attempt anything resembling a survey of the main problems generally collected under the name "philosophy of history." The division of the field into these two main parts, however, is so widely accepted and basic, that something approaching equal treatment for each of them will be offered.

Contemporary philosophers of history, with good reason, generally write with one eye on the neighboring field of philosophy of science. It may be helpful, therefore, to call the reader's attention to the fact that a corresponding division into speculative and critical parts will seldom be found in treatments of the latter field. What is generally called

---

[1] Maurice Mandelbaum's terms "material" and " formal" are also widely used to distinguish the two kinds of philosophy of history. See his "Some Neglected Philosophic Problems Regarding History," *Journal of Philosophy*, XLIX, No. 10 (May 8, 1952), 317. It should perhaps be pointed out, however, that not everything properly called "philosophy of history" falls easily into one of these two categories. See, for example, E. L. Fackenheim's metaphysical analysis of "historicity" in *Metaphysics and Historicity* (Milwaukee: Marquette University Press, 1961).

1

philosophy of science corresponds entirely to that part of the philosophy of history here called "critical"; it elucidates the concept and structure of scientific *inquiry*. The philosophical study of the system of nature itself, or cosmology, is now somewhat out of fashion. Where done, it is usually treated as part of general metaphysics.

It must be admitted, however, that the construction of speculative systems of history is also somewhat out of fashion. It was *Time* and *Life* magazines, rather than serious academic journals, which received Toynbee's *Study of History* with enthusiasm; and Hegel's philosophy of history is nowadays usually regarded, even by those who have never read a word of it, as a paradigm of how not to theorize about the past. Perhaps because an understanding of history matters so much to most of us, however, or because in a predominantly Judaic-Christian culture the expectation that history should be "meaningful" is so strong, speculative philosophy of history has still not quite achieved the fossil status often attributed to cosmology. It is studied (ostensibly at least) for its "insights," or for its elaboration of significant "viewpoints." And it is frequently, if uneasily, believed that whether we study the subject or not, we all in fact have an implicit philosophy of history. This volume will not attempt to defend any particular system, of the many which have been offered by philosophers (and quasi-philosophers) from Augustine to the present. Its aim will be rather to show the *kind* of thing such speculative systems are, to offer a broad classification of them, to distinguish some of the chief problems to which they purport to offer solutions, to sketch the main doctrines of a few of them, and to call attention to some of the difficulties they raise. This will be the subject matter of Chapters 5 through 8.

The earlier chapters will offer an introduction to critical philosophy of history through a discussion of representative problems. In explanation of the choice of problems to be treated, a further reference to the philosophy of science may be helpful. For the *raison d'être* of critical philosophy of history is very closely bound up with the question whether historical inquiry is, or is not, "scientific," in a sense in which physics, biology, psychology or even applied sciences like engineering are. If history is—or at any rate, ought to be—scientific in this sense, there is scarcely any need for a separate critique of historical inquiry. Historical method will presumably just be scientific method as applied to the special subject matter which interests historians; and history will be classified as a branch of social science. The chief focus of interest of critical philosophy of history, since the beginning of its intensive development less than a century ago, has been precisely on this question. Without entirely denying that it may have certain local peculiarities, one group of philosophers has argued that there are no *fundamental* peculiarities that would justify a separate critique of history. Those holding this position are nowadays often referred to as "positivists"; and despite certain misleading connotations of this term, it will be used for convenience of reference in what follows. Their opponents have frequently been called "idealists." [2] And although this may be to use philosophical terms with even less exactitude, it is true at least that a good deal of the inspiration for the claim that history is in important ways a discipline with aims, concepts, and methods of its own has come from idealist philosophers like Collingwood, Croce, Dilthey—and even Hegel.

My own belief is that there are, in fact, quite central features of historical inquiry which make it profoundly misleading to call history, without qualification, a science. If I did not think so, I should scarcely have thought it worthwhile to devote half a volume in the Foundations of Philosophy Series to critical philosophy of history. It has therefore seemed best to use the space available in the first half of this book to consider questions which bear directly on this issue, and which have been at the center of recent controversy in critical philosophy of history. The first is the question of the kind of understanding or explanation the historian tries to give of his subject matter, it being asserted by the idealists, and denied by the positivists, that this is different in concept from what is sought in scientific studies proper. The second is the question whether the conclusions historians seek to establish can be asserted with the kind of objectivity which scientists claim to achieve. Once again there is disagreement, the idealists tending to question the positivists' belief that they can be. These discussions will be followed by a consideration of the problem of causal judgment in history. Here issues already raised will appear again in a slightly different form.

It should perhaps be added that although I have declared myself, in a general way, with respect to the issues to be discussed, it will be the aim of the book to make the reader acquainted with some of the arguments which have been offered on both sides. In this connection, the footnoted references to recent articles and books will serve, in addition to the text, as the reader's introduction.

[2] For a criticism of the tendency to divide critical philosophers of history into idealists and positivists in this way, see Maurice Mandelbaum, "Historical Explanation: The Problem of 'Covering Laws,'" *History and Theory*, I, No. 3 (1961), 229-30.

HISTORICAL

UNDERSTANDING

2

Fact and
explanation
The chief task of critical philosophy of history, it might be said, is to clarify and analyze the "idea" of history. We may well begin, therefore, by asking what historical inquiry is about. At least ostensibly (although even this has not gone unchallenged) the concern of the historian is with the *past*. More specifically, it is, of course, with the *human* past; and some philosophers would make this latter limitation a matter of principle, on the ground that the concepts and methods historians employ are not applicable to natural events. Thus R. G. Collingwood calls Samuel Alexander to task for speaking of "the historicity" of all things.[1] Even if it is intelligible to speak of the "history" of a natural object, however, this is clearly not the sort of thing history, as we actually find it, is about. Natural occurrences may certainly be referred to in histories; but only insofar as they are thought to affect, or present problems to, those human beings whose story the historian seeks to tell. Two further limitations of scope might perhaps be mentioned at the outset, although they may be thought more controversial. The first is that history, as Collingwood and other idealist philosophers have always emphasized, is concerned primarily with the *activities* of human beings. Whether Queen Elizabeth had a sore throat on a given morning becomes an object of historical study only if it may have prevented her from attending a Privy Council meeting. This also illustrates the second limitation: that although, in a sense, history is concerned always with the activities of *individuals*, it is not concerned with them *as such*. An action does not become subject matter for a historian unless it has what Maurice Mandelbaum calls "societal significance." [2]

[1] *The Idea of History* (New York: Oxford University Press, 1956; a Galaxy book), p. 210.
[2] *The Problem of Historical Knowledge* (New York: Liveright Publishing Corp., 1938), pp. 9, 14.

4

If history is concerned with past human actions of societal significance, what is the *nature* of that concern? One obvious answer is: to find out what they were, to "establish the facts." This raises the first of the questions of critical philosophy of history which we shall deal with in this book. For it is surely the historian's task, it might be said, not only to establish the facts, but to *understand* them. And this will involve him in giving explanations.

There are theorists of history who would evade the problems with which we must now begin to deal by denying that historians ever do, or ought to, explain anything. History, they will say, is bound only to find out exactly what happened. If explanations are sought, they should be sought elsewhere: from the social sciences, perhaps, for which the historian provides raw "factual" material. Indeed, historians themselves sometimes take this line, rather than admit liability to give account of their mode of explanation. Such a claim, however, is belied by the most casual glance at what historians write. They constantly claim to "throw light on" or "make clear" what they are talking about; and their exposition is richly interlarded with such explanatory expressions as "since," "therefore," and "because." Little attention therefore need be paid to this curiously modest position.

Explanation and law   When historians *do* claim understanding, what form do their explanations take? What is their concept of a satisfactory explanation? One might assume that the nature of the subject matter might make special demands upon them in this connection. Positivist philosophers of history, however, deny the relevance of such considerations. To them the concept of explanation is subject-neutral: it is necessarily the same wherever explanation is successfully given. For its *clearest* exemplification, however, they advise us to look where thought itself is at its clearest: namely, to physical science. If historians ever do give genuine explanations, we may assume that in concept and structure they will closely approximate scientific ones.

Now scientific explanations themselves may be given at various levels of sophistication. It seems generally to be agreed, however, that insofar as they explain particular occurrences, they have one crucial feature in common: they render predictable what is explained by subsuming it under universal empirical laws. In ideal cases, such subsumption exhibits a deductive pattern: a statement asserting the occurrence of what is to be explained is shown to be logically deducible from statements setting forth certain antecedent conditions, together with certain empirically verified general laws. Even at the level of common sense, the same pattern obtains. If I wish to explain the falling of a slate off my roof, what I must refer to is the general law of gravitation, plus the antecedent condition that the slate, unfortunately, was unsupported. If I wish to explain the outbreak of the French Revolution, I must similarly outline conditions preceding it which, together with statements of appropriate laws, allow its occurrence to be deduced. Carl

Hempel, in an authoritative exposition of the position, puts it like this:

> Historical explanation, too, aims at showing that the event in question was not a "matter of chance," but was to be expected in view of certain antecedent or simultaneous conditions. The expectation referred to is not prophecy or divination, but rational scientific anticipation which rests on the assumption of general laws.[3]

In science, of course, the laws required for explanation would themselves be objects of discovery in the particular discipline concerned. In history, since the establishment of laws is not the purpose of the inquiry, those required for explanation would have to be derived from elsewhere—possibly from the social sciences, or even from that general experience of the world we sometimes refer to as common sense. The historian, as C. B. Joynt and Nicholas Rescher have expressed it, "is not a *producer* of general laws, but a *consumer* of them." [4] This question of origin, however, is not directly relevant to the positivist claim. For that claim is essentially a *conceptual* one. What it asserts is a logical or conceptual connection between having knowledge of laws and being able to give explanations that are defensible. And it is argued that what is true of explanation generally must be true also of *historical* explanation.

Now there is something very persuasive about this account of the nature of explanation. Whether it states a sufficient condition of explaining something, even in science, may perhaps be doubted. But it is tempting to believe that it states at least a *necessary* condition of doing so. Alan Donagan has offered the following "proof" of the deductive thesis.[5] If what we give in explanation of an event does not rule out the possibility of that event's failing to occur, then we can scarcely claim that we know why in that particular case it *did* occur: why in that case, in other words, the possibility of its not occurring was not realized instead. The only way we can rule out such a possibility is by arguing that

---

[3] "The Function of General Laws in History," reprinted in *Theories of History*, ed. Patrick Gardiner (New York: Free Press of Glencoe, Inc., 1959), pp. 348-49. The discussion of Hempel's thesis that follows derives largely from my *Laws and Explanation in History* (New York: Oxford University Press, 1957). For more sophisticated statements of the nature of scientific explanation, see Hempel's *Philosophy of Natural Science* and Richard Rudner's *Philosophy of Social Science*, Prentice-Hall Foundations of Philosophy Series.

[4] "The Problem of Uniqueness in History," *History and Theory*, I, No. 2 (1961), 154.

[5] "Explanation in History," reprinted in *Theories of History*, ed. Gardiner, p. 430. Donagan denies, however, that this proves the full positivist thesis that explanatory deduction must employ empirical laws. Further developments of Donagan's views, which unfortunately cannot be considered in this introduction, can be found in his *The Later Philosophy of R. G. Collingwood* (New York: Oxford University Press, 1962), pp. 173ff, and a forthcoming article in *History and Theory* entitled "Historical Explanation: The Popper-Hempel Theory Reconsidered." For a spirited defense of the full Hempelian claim, see May Brodbeck, "Explanation, Prediction, and 'Imperfect' Knowledge," in *Scientific Explanation, Space, and Time*, ed. Herbert Feigl and Grover Maxwell, Minnesota Studies in the Philosophy of Science, Vol. III (Minneapolis: University of Minnesota Press, 1962), pp. 231-72.

the event *had* to occur: that it *necessarily* occurred. And that is what the deductive requirement of scientific explanation insures. Most positivists would add that this requirement can be satisfied only by appeal to general laws.

It is one thing, of course, to state an ideal of explanation. It is quite another to decide how strictly to apply it in assessment of the work of historians. Hempel himself did not say categorically that nothing falling short of the requirements stated can be counted as explanation at all. The obvious difficulty in history is that the results of doing so might force us all the way back to the position indicated at the beginning of this chapter: that historians never explain—although our grounds now would be, not that they do not wish to, but rather that they are unable to. For historians almost never mention universal laws when they give explanations of events; and it is highly doubtful whether in the vast majority of cases they could even claim to know such laws. Donagan has argued that every general statement formulated for incorporation into a historical explanation turns out to be either not universal (since it contains qualifications of various kinds as a hedge against counter-instances) or not true—unless its defenders take advantage of still a third possibility and protect it against criticism by making it covertly tautological.[6] The infrequent references to generalizations which one *does* find in the work of historians lend credence to such a claim.

Hempel's own response to this difficulty was twofold. On the one hand he suggested that historians, although they usually give no more than approximations to scientifically warranted explanations (they offer only "explanation sketches"), nevertheless may be defended insofar as they are at least guided by the scientific ideal. On the other hand, he admitted that even in natural science, universal laws and deductive relations often have to give place to probability hypotheses and inductive relations; for the only laws available are often not universal but statistical. Historical explanations, he assumed, could be represented as conforming especially to the latter, weaker version of the scientific model.

It might surely be argued, however, that such easing of the requirements of the scientific model bears the marks of expediency rather than principle. A theory that begins by elaborating the essential meaning of explanation a priori, rather than trying to discover what the practitioners of the discipline concerned themselves call explanation, is surely on weak ground when it relaxes its requirements in the face of difficulties of application. The apparent need for such a move may well prepare us, at any rate, to give serious consideration to alternative accounts of what historians are trying to do when they explain, especially to accounts that are grounded in contrary principles. It is such accounts which idealist philosophers of history like Michael Oakeshott and R. G. Collingwood have claimed to give. Both base their objections to the

---

[6] See his forthcoming article cited in footnote 5.

scientific model on a conception of the nature of the historian's subject matter. For Oakeshott the crucial point is the historian's concern with a unique, nonrepeatable series of events. For Collingwood it is his interest in rational human action. Let us look briefly at each of these positions.

"The moment historical facts are regarded as instances of general laws," Oakeshott declares, "history is dismissed." [7] To attempt so to regard them, he continues, is to ignore a *presupposition* of historical inquiry; it is to transform a historical way of investigating past events into a scientific one. For Oakeshott, the impossibility of explaining historical events on the scientific model is thus not simply an empirical one—a matter of mere practical difficulty. What he means by calling this a presupposition of history, however, perhaps itself requires some explanation.

Oakeshott's point appears to be roughly as follows. It is a commonplace that science is concerned with the general features of the world: the scientist has no interest in individual things or events as such. This is most obviously true in such highly developed sciences as physics and chemistry, where laws and theories are elaborated to account for what we experience. It is the laws and theories, rather than what exemplifies them, that are the objects of concern. A similar situation obtains, however, even at the level of science called "natural history" (in a sense of "history" quite different from the one historians use). For a botanist, a particular specimen is of interest only insofar as it is a representative of its kind. But in history, it may be claimed, the situation is very different. The historian is interested in *the* French Revolution or *the* execution of Charles I—individual historical events—not in revolutions and executions as such. To study these events as examples of their kind may be perfectly legitimate and interesting; but it scarcely represents a typically historical approach to what happened. For the historian's interest in such events will not be confined to those aspects or features which they shared with other revolutions and executions. He will want to study them in all their uniqueness and particularity.

Here we seem to have a direct confrontation of doctrines. For laws, as Hempel makes clear, apply to *kinds* of events, not to unique occurrences. To explain an event on the positivist model, the historian will consequently have to classify his object of study as an event of a certain kind. But if such a procedure would involve, for Oakeshott, "the complete destruction of history," what is his alternative account of the way historians proceed? "The only explanation of change relevant or possible in history," he says roundly, "is simply a complete account of change. History accounts *for* change by means of a full account *of* change." The historian's ideal of explanation is thus "the exhibition of a world of events intrinsically related to one another in which no *lacuna*

---

[7] *Experience and Its Modes* (London: Cambridge University Press, 1933), p. 154.

is tolerated." [8] For Oakeshott, "the method of the historian is never to explain by means of generalization." Historical understanding is always achieved rather "by means of greater and more complete detail."

Against this sort of stand, Hempelians have generally offered two sorts of objections. They have argued, first, that although historical events are in one sense unique and unrepeatable (no two events are identical "as they actually occurred"), the philosophical use to which idealists like Oakeshott wish to put this contention is not legitimate. For exactly the same could be said of the events natural scientists study; and it is not denied that laws and theories apply to them. The idealist response to this, however, has really already been given. For the reason the scientist has no problem about the uniqueness of his events, it might be said, is that he is not interested in them as unique, whereas the historian allegedly is. But this brings us to the second argument. We must remember, Hempelians will point out, that the concern of critical philosophy of history is to elucidate the idea of history *as an inquiry*. Even if historical events really *are* in themselves unique, in a sense which rules out the applicability of laws, the question is whether in historical inquiry they can be known as such, and hence whether historians can sensibly be said to be interested in them as such. It should be clear, at any rate, that they cannot be *described* as such; for historical description, like scientific or any other, must use general concepts; and these, whether we like to admit it or not, necessarily classify what is being talked about. In a type of inquiry which is conducted in the presence of its object, it may make sense to claim that we can know, through sense perception, more than can adequately be expressed in language. But the objects of historical inquiry are past and gone. What is present to the historian's senses is only *evidence* for them.

This rebuttal has considerable force. Its force, however, should not be overestimated for the settling of the present issue. For it cannot claim in itself to *establish* the positivist account of explanation as valid for history; it can claim only to set aside a fallacious objection to that account. It very properly reminds us that *what* a historian explains (if he is clearheaded enough to ask a precise question) must be specifiable in general terms. A historian who insists that he can explain "the French Revolution," without being willing to say what it is about the French Revolution he is going to account for, will simply fail to communicate. Whether, having specified this in language, he can properly claim to have provided an explanation, without showing that it follows, in accordance with *laws*, from other events similarly specified in general terms, is a question which still remains to be decided.

Oakeshott's claim to have shown that laws are not necessary rests chiefly upon his use of the notion of "continuity" as a criterion of understanding in history. In opposition to the positivist model he offers what might be called a "continuous series" model of explanation. The

[8] *Ibid.*, p. 143.

historian may claim to understand one event's succeeding another, it would seem, when he can "fill in" the intervening events. To explain the outbreak of a revolution in France in 1789, for example, it is not enough to cite the corruption of the nobility by Louis XIV. This would not be enough even if we could appeal with any plausibility to some such generalization as "Whenever a ruling class loses its sense of political responsibility, a revolution follows within a century." A historical explanation would scarcely have been given unless the "connection" between the one condition and the other were *shown*. And this would involve a detailed tracing of the relations between the classes in France throughout the period.

The kind of objection a positivist would bring against this is not difficult to imagine. He might readily concede that it is characteristic of historical explanation to trace the continuity between apparently unrelated events in such a way. But he would ask exactly what Oakeshott means by the continuity of such a series; he would ask what renders the explanatory events "intrinsically related." His own elucidation of the notion of a continuous series would make use of the very Hempelian model Oakeshott is attacking. Continuity in events, he would say, can mean only that each component of the series follows "naturally" upon its predecessor—that is, can be seen to be necessitated by it in accordance with relevant general laws. If Oakeshott has some other sense of continuity in mind, some other meaning of a "relation" between events, then he should make it clear.

It must be admitted that Oakeshott fails to do this. That is not to say that his critique of the positivist theory completely misses the mark as it stands. For the notion that continuity in a historical series is established simply by applying the Hempelian model at every step clearly will not do. On such a criterion, for example, the relation between the court policy of Louis XIV and the outbreak of the Revolution would itself have been certifiable as one of continuity (given the generalization previously cited), whereas it is almost certain that no historian would so regard it. Thus in insisting that historical understanding depends upon the reduction of such sequences to a detailed series of "understandable" steps, Oakeshott's theory appears to make an important point. The acceptance of even this part of his claim would require the denial, at any rate, that subsumption under law constitutes a *sufficient* condition of giving an explanation in history. But the question remains: if this is not the criterion of historical "connectedness," what *is* the historian's criterion? On this question, R. G. Collingwood has considerably more to say.

The rationality of actions   Collingwood bases his opposition to the positivist account less on history's concern with unique occurrences (which he would, however, not deny) than on its having to explain, not natural events, but the actions of human beings who are at least to some extent free to order their activities in accordance with the demands of reason. Like most idealists, Collingwood draws a sharp distinction between the ways in which the two sorts of subject matters are to be understood. To use his own terminology, natural events can be explained only from the "outside," and this involves the kind of procedures set forth in the positivist theory. Historical actions, however, are not "mere events"; they have an "inside" or "thought-side." Their explanation requires the discovery of the thought of the agent which the action as a whole expresses. According to Collingwood, to explain an action by reference to the thought of the agent does not require its subsumption under general law. In *The Idea of History*, he put the point this way:

> For science, the event is discovered by perceiving it, and the further search for its cause is conducted by assigning it to its class and determining the relation between that class and others. For history, the object to be discovered is not the mere event, but the thought expressed in it. To discover that thought is already to understand it.[9]

What Collingwood appears to be claiming here is that there can be a relationship between the thought of a historical agent and what that agent does which renders his action understandable. We must ask what kind of thought Collingwood envisaged here, and what its relation to the historical action had to be. His answer to these questions is contained in his doctrine that to understand an action the historian must "re-think" or "re-enact" the agent's thought in his own mind. This may appear a somewhat formidable notion. Collingwood's meaning, however, comes out clearly enough if we look at the way he applies it to examples. Suppose, he says, that a historian of Rome is studying the Theodosian Code, and has before him an edict of an emperor. What must he do to achieve historical understanding of the edict?

> In order to do that he must envisage the situation with which the emperor was trying to deal, and he must envisage it as that emperor envisaged it. Then he must see for himself, just as if the emperor's situation were his own, how such a situation might be dealt with; he must see the possible alternatives, and the reasons for choosing one rather than another; and thus he must go through the process which the emperor went through in deciding on this particular course. Thus he is re-enacting in his own mind the experience of the emperor; and only insofar as he does this has he any historical knowledge, as distinct from a merely philological knowledge, of the meaning of the edict.[10]

Clearly the kinds of thoughts which Collingwood's theory requires are those which could enter the practical deliberations of an agent trying to decide what his line of action should be. They would include such things as the agent's conception of the facts of his situation, the purposes he wishes to achieve in acting, his knowledge of means that might be

---

[9] P. 214. The interpretation of Collingwood's views that follows is elaborated at greater length in my "Historical Understanding as Re-thinking," *University of Toronto Quarterly*, XXVII, No. 2 (January, 1958), 200-215.

[10] *The Idea of History*, p. 283.

adopted, any scruples he might have about adopting them—anything that could be a consideration to be taken into account. The relation such thoughts must have to the action is that of providing a reason for doing it. When the historian can see that the agent's beliefs, purposes, principles, etc., give him a reason for doing what he did, then he can claim to understand the action. The kind of understanding thus achieved, it might be argued, is different in *concept* from that sought on the scientific model. For the latter endeavors to make clear, in the light of the circumstances, the *inevitability* (or, at least, the high probability) of what was done. The former—which we might perhaps call "rational" explanation—tries to make clear its *point* or *rationale*.

In insisting that the historian must re-think the agent's thoughts, what Collingwood is claiming is that the point of his action cannot be grasped without a piece of vicarious practical reasoning on the part of the historian. The latter, on considering the agent's thoughts, must see that, from the agent's own point of view, what he did really was *the thing to do*. Doubtless, Collingwood often puts this point obscurely. In order to understand an action, he declares, "it is necessary to 'know what someone else is thinking,' not only in the sense of knowing the same object that he knows, but in the further sense of knowing the act by which he knows it." And again, "the act of thinking can be studied only as an act." [11] The general idea that the historian must be able to "follow" the agent's reasoning is clear enough, however. If the attempt to re-think the agent's thought-action complex in this way breaks down—as Collingwood admits it has in the case of certain early Roman emperors—then we have a dark spot, an unintelligibility, a failure to explain.

Objections to Collingwood's theory   A number of objections have been made to Collingwood's account of such explanation. One very common one is that even if it were otherwise sound, its scope is very limited. Few actions of historical agents had a "thought-side" in the sense of being done for reasons consciously entertained; and those that did often involved irrational ways of thinking which it would be quite impossible to "follow" in the sense Collingwood appears to have in mind. To this it is often added that rational explanations would, in any case, be limited to the actions of individuals, and would be inapplicable to nations or institutions, movements or conditions, which historians spend so much of their time talking about.

Few Collingwoodians would regard this range of objections as very damaging, however. As Collingwood himself points out, a thought not fully articulated by the agent to himself may still make what was done rationally intelligible. Collingwood's theory does not depend on a view of "thought" which limits it to the content of an internal monologue. What it asserts is a criterion of intelligibility for actions; and this, it might be argued, will be the same even for explanations in terms of

[11] *Ibid.*, pp. 288, 293.

"unconscious" thoughts. The claim that Collingwood's analysis is inapplicable to actions which are not fully rational also requires further examination. For there are many sorts of cases falling under this general description which *can* be given Collingwoodian explanations. A person may act hastily, for example, or he may act for foolish goals. In neither case is rational understanding, as Collingwood conceives it, ruled out; for we can still follow the agent's practical deliberations from the standpoint of what he *did* take into account. What *is* excluded is rational understanding of an action which is judged to have been done contrary to good reasons known to the agent, or of one in which the agent was so confused that it is impossible to "follow" the connection between what he believed and what he did. As for the alleged limitation of the theory to individual actions, it is arguable that in history, as our discussion of Oakeshott's views has suggested, the ideal explanation, even of group phenomena, involves reduction to the explanation of what relevant individuals do. If this is so, the scope of Collingwood's theory, although narrower than the whole range of historians' concerns, is by no means limited to "drum and trumpet" or "Gladstone and Disraeli" types of history.

An objection which comes closer to the core of Collingwood's claims fastens on what he says about the need for re-enactment. In elaborating an "empathetic" or "projective" account of understanding, it is argued, he mistakes a psychological fact for a methodological principle. Hempel has offered a lucid and typical critique of all empathy theories along this line.[12] That actions in history are at least sometimes to be explained by reference to the agent's thoughts, Hempel does not question. But the projection involved, say, in putting oneself at the standpoint of a Roman emperor, he regards simply as a method of arriving at an explanatory hypothesis. The fact that such a procedure is often employed by historians, he would claim, throws no light whatever on the *structure* of the eventual explanations they give. For this hypothesis, once it is articulated, will assume the form of a statement of necessary connection between an agent's having a certain thought and acting in a certain way. That is, it asserts a psychological law. If the laws suggested by empathetic procedures are seldom worthy of the name, Hempel would add, this is because historians seldom submit them to the test of further verification. The explanations offered, however, will be in the same way, and to the same degree, defective.

Defenders of Collingwood are bound to regard such an objection as completely misunderstanding his meaning. In insisting on re-thinking, they will say, it was not his intention to describe a way of finding out certain elusive facts—the thoughts of historical agents, or the empirical connections between them and overt activities. It was his intention, rather, as has been observed already, to call attention to the criterion of intelligibility or connectedness historians employ. To be understood,

[12] "The Function of General Laws in History," *op. cit.*, pp. 352-53.

an action need not be referred to a thought from which it follows in accordance with a psychological law. To resolve puzzlement it is enough to show that it follows "rationally." In some cases it may indeed be said to follow with rational *necessity*; for agents sometimes have "compelling" reasons for doing what they do. This does not, however, entail a necessary connection between thought and action of the kind Hempel has in mind. It does not follow from the fact that an agent has "compelling" reasons to act, and knows it, that he will in fact do what they require— although if he does so we will claim to understand his doing so. In this connection, it might be noted that although Collingwood does not argue from any metaphysical assertion of human free will as premise, his theory of explanation is at least *compatible* with the truth of libertarianism. The positivist theory is not.

The most incisive positivist argument against the view here attributed to Collingwood harks back to Donagan's proof of the deductive thesis. It concedes that we may indeed need to know that an agent had good reason if we are going to claim understanding of what he did. But this, it will be contended, is only a necessary, not a sufficient, condition of validly making such a claim. For unless we know that the doing of the action follows necessarily upon the agent's having that reason—together, perhaps, with certain further specifiable conditions—we do not know why his action was in fact performed rather than not performed. Since (on Collingwood's theory, at any rate) its not being performed would have been quite consistent with the agent's having the reason he did, reference to the latter cannot be a *complete* explanation of its actual performance. According to Hempel, to be complete, the explanation "would have to include a further assumption, to the effect that at the time in question [the agent] was a rational agent, and was thus disposed to do what was appropriate in the given situation." [13] The explanation would thus be dependent on the truth of some such empirical generalization as: "A rational agent, when in a situation of kind C, will invariably (or with high probability) do X," where for C and X we can substitute statements of the agent's reasons and of his action respectively.

Two likely lines of reply to this sort of objection are open to Collingwoodians. The first would raise a doubt about regarding general statements like the one cited as *empirical* generalizations. Such statements as to what a rational agent would or would not do, it might be said, simply elucidate the notion of rational action. They are expressions of the criteria we apply to an agent in calling him rational, rather than reports of our discoveries as to what people, already classified as rational, in fact do. It is an essential feature of the scientific model, however, that the generalizations which are required for explanation should be empirical ones. The second line of reply centers on the notion of a disposition to behave rationally. Collingwoodians would deny that it is neces-

[13] "Reasons and Covering Laws in Historical Explanation," in *Philosophy and History*, ed. Sidney Hook (New York: New York University Press, 1963), p. 155.

sary, in order to claim understanding of a particular action, to know that the agent is rational in the sense that he always, or in a certain proportion of cases, does what reason requires. As long as we have reason to think that he *can* act so—that he is a rational agent in the sense of being able to choose what to do, and able to appreciate the force of the various considerations presented to him—then if he acts for good reason we can claim to understand his action (although not necessarily to know the answer to a further question why he acted rationally at all). The demand for further "completion" of the explanation appears to be a demand for what we probably cannot get, and in any case do not need.

Some revisions
of the
positivist
theory

Both of the reactions against the positivist analysis which have been noted take their stand on the theoretical inappropriateness of such analysis in view of the nature of the historian's subject matter. There are many philosophers, however, who would agree that the positivist model is unacceptable as it stands, while questioning the kinds of arguments urged against it by Oakeshott and Collingwood. They would endeavor rather to emend that model, to bring it more closely into line with actual historical practice, while keeping at least a vestige of its central claim intact. As we have noted, Hempel himself was willing to do this to the extent of allowing an inductive as well as a deductive version of the model. But much more drastic modifications than this have often been proposed, and of these, three particularly interesting ones may be noted briefly here. What holds them together is their agreement that some kind of generalization is required to complete a historical explanation. Where they differ is in the account they give of how far, and in what way, such a generalization may deviate from the universal law of Hempel's original theory, while still performing an explanatory function.

The first is a view put forward by Michael Scriven.[14] According to Scriven, a generalization may be explanatory without being strictly universal: that is, an explanation would not be invalidated necessarily by our finding counterinstances for the generalization which warrants it. It matters very much, however, how these counterinstances are to be conceived. For Scriven would deny that a mere *statistical* law explains what falls under it—where this means any law asserting a general connection, not between all cases of certain kinds, but only between a certain proportion of them. Against Hempel, and in the spirit of Donagan's "proof," Scriven argues that a statistical law connecting, say, certain economic conditions with revolutions, would tell us nothing at all about a particular revolutionary outbreak that followed such conditions; at most, it would explain why, in the long run, the proportion of outbreaks under

[14] "Truisms as the Grounds for Historical Explanations," in *Theories of History*, ed. Gardiner, pp. 464ff. Scriven has developed his view further in "New Issues in the Logic of Explanation," in *Philosophy and History*, ed. Hook, pp. 339ff. For further discussion of suggested modifications of the scientific model, see my "The Historical Explanation of Actions Reconsidered," in the same volume.

those conditions was what it was. But there are some less-than-universal laws, he adds, which are *neither* universal nor statistical. They formulate what happens in "normal circumstances." According to Scriven, our common-sense knowledge of the world is almost entirely made up of such "normic" generalizations. And history, which is an extension of such knowledge, commonly employs them in making what happened understandable. An example of such a generalization in history would be: "Rulers who cannot administer the territories they have already do not normally attack their neighbors' lands." Such a generalization could be appealed to in explaining why William the Conqueror did not invade Scotland.

Two difficulties in Scriven's proposal might be mentioned. The first concerns the oddity of his nonstatistical concept of a norm. Such a notion, it might be argued, is only a vague and replaceable way of talking about a statistical regularity we have not yet fully worked out. Scriven's remarks about the inadequacy of statistical explanation, however, seem to imply that normic regularities are *essentially* different from statistical ones—their explanatory power actually depending upon their being irreducible to statisticals. The second difficulty arises out of the very miscellaneous collection of generalizations that he sweeps into the normic class. At least some seem to state evaluative norms of behavior rather than *empirical* regularities. And it is tempting to say that explanations using these, since they certify what was done as conforming to a *standard* of behavior, are really rational explanations in disguise. The explanation suggested for William's noninvasion of Scotland, for example, might plausibly be interpreted this way. The explanation reminds us how pointless that invasion would have been.

A second kind of nonuniversal law which has been proposed to replace unavailable universal ones in historical cases is what Nicholas Rescher and Olaf Helmer have called a "limited" or "restricted" generalization.[15] This is conceived, unlike Scriven's, as without counterinstances, but as holding only within a limited period of time or in a limited geographical area. An example would be "Pre-Revolutionary French naval officers were drawn from the noble classes," asserted in explanation of a certain appointment's being made. The notion that historians may explain satisfactorily by using generalizations of this kind, it might be noted, accords well with their own practice and their conception of their commitments. No historian would object to the claim that his explanation required a deep knowledge of "the period." But he does not want to stand committed, by an explanation he gives of an eighteenth century event, to the truth of a generalization which is applicable, say, to the Middle Ages—about which professional modesty may require him to disclaim much knowledge.

Once again, two difficulties might be mentioned. The first is the

[15] "On the Epistemology of the Inexact Sciences," *Management Science*, VI, No. 1 (October, 1959), 25-40. See also C. B. Joynt and Nicholas Rescher, "On Explanation in History," *Mind*, LXVIII, No. 271 (July, 1959), 383-87.

question whether the spatio-temporally limited generalizations envisaged by Rescher and Helmer deserve the name "law" at all. For they may appear rather to be mere summative general statements, referring to finite collections of events or conditions (like "All the beans in this bag are red"). To this it would be replied that although they are not *universal* laws, they are not mere summative statements of fact, either. For they govern instances as yet unexamined, and (more importantly) they have counterfactual force, implying something about instances that might have existed but did not. The generalization given, for example, warrants the conclusion that if the French had decided to expand their officer cadre, the new recruits would also have been drawn from the nobility. If we accept this, however, we encounter a second difficulty. For the question arises, how we can know that a certain limited generalization, with implications as strong as these, is true. And the answer of Rescher and Helmer appears to be that we test it by seeing that it follows from the "conditions of the period"—presumably in accordance with universal laws. Explanation by limited generalization might thus be regarded by a Hempelian as covertly dependent on scientific explanation in the full-blown sense. Since explanation by limited generalization was originally proposed because knowledge of universal laws could not be claimed, this is scarcely a satisfactory conclusion.

A third modification of the original model, at one stage urged by Donagan, asserts the adequacy of a generalization which applies, not to a type or kind of person or event, but to a named *individual*.[16] A case in point would be the explanation of Disraeli's attack on Peel by reference to his political ambition, or to the depredations of the Danes by reference to their being plunderers. All explanations of individual behavior by reference to the "dispositions" of the individual persons would fall into this class. Once again it is easy to see how attractive the modification would be to practicing historians, who are perfectly familiar with the need to discover, without reference to more general theories, what is *characteristic* of the more important agents, institutions, or groups they study. Such "individual" explanations, it might be added, can also be given of natural events. I might explain the behavior of my car, for example, by reference to its sluggishness in cold weather—without implying anything about other cars or knowing why it is sluggish in cold weather (although I may *believe* this could be explained with the aid of general laws). Scientists, however, who unlike historians and drivers lack interest in the peculiarities of individual things, would be unlikely to use this sort of explanation.

The chief difficulty with the claim that "individual" explanation constitutes a separate type, logically independent of the Hempelian scheme, arises out of the logical complexity of most human dispositional

---

[16] "Explanation in History," *op. cit.*, pp. 428ff. Donagan has modified his position considerably in the later work cited in footnote 5. Something like the original position is defended by Patrick Gardiner in *The Nature of Historical Explanation* (New York: Oxford University Press, 1952).

characteristics. As Jonathan Cohen has pointed out, human dispositions, like being ambitious, envious, or angry, have many (and perhaps an indefinite number) of kinds of manifestations or expressions.[17] A simple disposition, like the tendency to squint in a bright light, can be asserted of an individual on evidence of his past behavior, assuming no more than the validity of inductive argument in general. But complex dispositions can only be asserted without further assumption if we have verified independently *every possible kind* of manifestation for the individual concerned. Even if such verification is theoretically possible, it is unlikely to be common in actual historical inquiry. It may therefore be claimed (as in the case of appeal to limited generalizations) that dispositional explanations in history normally *would* commit the investigator to certain further assumptions of a universal form—in particular, about the likelihood that a person who manifests a disposition in one way would manifest it also in another.

Other kinds   In even a brief account of the issues surrounding the problem of
of explanation   historical explanation, some mention should perhaps be made of
                      another source of difficulty for the so-called "scientific" theory as it stands. This is the contention that the latter, although it claims to offer a *general* account of explanation, takes cognizance only of explanations of why things in fact happened, whereas historians often offer explanations of quite different kinds, some of which are not intended to answer "why" questions at all. The acceptance of the Hempelian model as at least an obvious ideal, with a consequent tendency to fit historical explanations as far as possible into its pattern, may thus completely obscure the kind of intelligibility the historian often seeks to discover in his subject matter. The two sorts of procedures which will be noted in concluding this chapter would generally be called explanations by historians. It is plausible to argue, however, that they fall completely outside the analysis so far presented.

The first might be called "explaining how something could be so, in spite of a presumption to the contrary." [18] This is a very common procedure where conclusions assume narrative form, as they do so often in history. Certain expectations are aroused by a certain train of events: an institution, working well, gives every promise of weathering a crisis, but suddenly breaks down; a policy that appears to be the rational course for an individual to follow is suddenly abandoned. In the face of such an unexpected train of events, the historian's question, rather than "Why did this happen?" (meaning "What *made* it happen?") may well be "How could this have happened?" And such a question can be completely answered by rebutting the presumption that it could not have happened: by showing that, contrary to first appearances, there was no reason why it should not have happened.

[17] Review, *Philosophical Quarterly*, X, No. 39 (April, 1960), 191.
[18] For a discussion of this kind of explanation, see my "Explanatory Narrative in History," *Philosophical Quarterly*, IV, No. 14 (January, 1954), 15-27.

In such cases of explanation, it should be clear that, since the problem is not to show that what happened had to happen, there is no need to subsume the occurrence under a law, universal or otherwise. What is needed is a demonstration of the *possibility* of the event by removing the basis for the expectation that it would not happen. It is true that a historian will sometimes not rest satisfied with such an explanation. He may go on to ask *why* the unexpected happened. The point is simply that he *need* not do this in order to give an explanation which is formally complete, regarded as an answer to its own type of question. The relation between the answers to such "how" and "why" questions is not that of first approximation to complete explanation, or of defective to perfect explanation. It is rather that of two kinds of explanation, given in response to different questions, which may in fact sometimes succeed each other in historical work.

W. B. Gallie, in discussing the nature of "genetic" explanation, of which he considers historical explanation to be one type, makes a somewhat similar point.[19] Historical explanations, he argues, are generally attempts to set forth certain crucial or especially interesting *necessary* conditions of events; they make no attempt to discover *sufficient* conditions. The historian's narrative attains explanatory status and the continuity which understanding requires when he shows that "but for" a certain condition—perhaps a surprising one—what happened would not have occurred. The historian's task, in other words, is constantly to discover the conditions making possible what actually happened. But although this may be correct as far as it goes, it is arguable that Gallie here gives an incomplete analysis of the historian's procedure. For he does not want to claim that ideally the historian would set down *all* the necessary conditions, yet he gives no account of what makes reference to one necessary condition explanatory by contrast with another. Such a difficulty does not arise for the account previously given of "explaining how something could have happened." For the condition which is explanatory is clearly the one which rebuts the presumption that what happened could not have occurred.

A second kind of procedure generally referred to as explanation in history, although also sometimes as "interpretation," is explanation of what an event "really was," or what it "amounts to." [20] Once again, this is to be distinguished from explaining why the event occurred. The operative notion in such cases is less that of discovering necessary and sufficient conditions than of relating parts, at first not seen to be such, to a whole of some kind. Thus the historian explains a host of occurrences in fifteenth century Italy as a "Renaissance"; he explains a series of incidents in eighteenth century France as a "Revolution." In doing this he undoubtedly traces connections between individual events, and

[19] "Explanations in History and the Genetic Sciences," reprinted in *Theories of History*, ed. Gardiner, pp. 386, 402.

[20] This is discussed more fully in my " 'Explaining What' in History," in *Theories of History*, ed. Gardiner, pp. 403-8.

these connections may be of various kinds—some might even be the kind envisaged in the scientific model. But the burden of explanation is in the synthesis of the parts into a new whole—a procedure that Lincoln Reis and P. O. Kristeller have called "vertical" by contrast with "horizontal" interpretation.[21]

It appears to be this sort of thing that W. H. Walsh also had in mind when he spoke of historians throwing light on their subject matter by "colligating" events under "appropriate conceptions." [22] For in both the cases cited above, the historian's synthesis is expressed by means of an organizing concept. Historical insight often shows itself in the choice of such concepts, where the notions (for example, "Renaissance") are plainly analogical. Such colligation, it might be added, is no artistic ornament to historical inquiry: it is of its essence. It has no logical similarity, however, to explanation on the scientific model, as positivists have generally represented it.

[21] "Some Remarks on the Method of History," *Journal of Philosophy*, XL, No. 9 (April 29, 1943), 240ff.

[22] *Philosophy of History: An Introduction* (New York: Harper & Row, Publishers, 1960; a Torchbook), pp. 59-64; also "The Intelligibility of History," *Philosophy*, XVII, No. 66 (April, 1942), 133-35.

HISTORICAL OBJECTIVITY

3

Historical
relativism

In the preceding chapter we discussed some of the issues raised by the question: What kind of understanding or intelligibility does the historian look for in his subject matter? Although what was said could scarcely be represented as a full theory of historical explanation, considerations did emerge which might well make us wary of assuming that the historian's ideal conforms very closely to what is widely taken to be the pattern of scientific explanation. In the present chapter, we turn to a question which will drive us to consider other aspects of the historian's task than the purely explanatory one. This is the question of the extent to which historians can legitimately claim the status of "objective truth" for the conclusions they characteristically reach; whether they can claim, in the oft-quoted words of Ranke, to reconstruct the past *exactly as it was*. Those who assert that they can, we may once again call "positivists"—or, possibly, "objectivists." Those who deny this possibility, following common practice, we may refer to as "relativists." [1]

According to W. H. Walsh, the problem of historical objectivity is "at once the most important and the most baffling in critical philosophy of history." [2] Certainly the reasons why history has been said *not* to be objective are bewilderingly many and various. According to the American historian, Charles Beard, for example, history is not objective because

[1] For a general discussion of historical relativism by an objectivist, see Mandelbaum, *The Problem of Historical Knowledge*. The term "relativism," like "positivism" and "idealism," is in some ways unfortunate, but it provides a convenient label for present purposes.

[2] *Philosophy of History: An Introduction*, p. 94. Chapter V of Walsh's book offers an excellent discussion of the problem of objectivity, using a wider definition of "objective" as "such as to warrant acceptance by all who seriously investigate" (p. 96).

the historian cannot "observe" his subject matter as a chemist can; because his documentation of the past is fragmentary; because he must select even from this "partial record"; because he must "arrange" his materials in reporting his results; because in employing organizing concepts he imposes a "structure" on the past which it never really had; because the events he is interested in involve "ethical and aesthetic considerations"; because no historian, in any case, can bring to his work a "neutral mind." [3] This would appear to be a very miscellaneous set of worries, to say the least, and it is far from evident that they are brought together with any one clear meaning of the term "objective" in mind. In this chapter, in order to keep discussion manageable, only one of the several issues generally raised by relativists like Beard will be discussed: the question whether historical inquiry must be regarded as nonobjective because it involves "ethical and aesthetic considerations"—or (as it is often put) because it requires "value judgment" on the part of the historian. This interpretation of the problem of objectivity, although it is not the only important one, has in fact provided the framework for a good deal of recent discussion by both historians and philosophers of history. At the end of the chapter attention will be called to one other important sense of the term.

When historians themselves discuss the question whether history can be objective, they are notoriously pessimistic. Thus Carl Becker insists that "the historian cannot eliminate the personal equation." [4] And Beard declares: "Whatever acts of purification the historian may perform, he yet remains human, a creature of time, place, circumstance, interests, predilections, culture"; going on to observe: "No amount of renunciation could have made Andrew D. White into a Frederick Jackson Turner, or either of them into a neutral mirror." [5] As these pronouncements suggest, however, historians tend to interpret the question in a quasi-psychological way, They emphasize the *difficulty* of eliminating "prejudices," or they represent "bias" as an amiable, if ubiquitous, fact of human nature.[6] The interest of critical philosophy of history in this matter will clearly not be to discover simply whether history, as generally pursued, is *in fact* a value-neutral inquiry. The question will be rather whether it is so in concept or "idea." As Ernest Nagel has put it, the question is whether the historian's value scheme is "not only causally influential upon his inquiry, but is *logically* involved, both in his standards of validity as well as in the meaning of his statements." [7] If this

[3] "That Noble Dream," reprinted in *The Varieties of History*, ed. Fritz Stern (Cleveland: World Publishing Co., 1956; a Meridian book), pp. 323-25.

[4] "What Are Historical Facts?" reprinted in *The Philosophy of History in Our Time*, ed. Hans Meyerhoff (Garden City: Doubleday & Company, Inc., 1959; an Anchor book), p. 131.

[5] "That Noble Dream," *op. cit.*, p. 324.

[6] See, for example, some parts of G. M. Trevelyan's "Bias in History," *History*, XXXII, No. 115 (March, 1947), 1-15.

[7] "The Logic of Historical Analysis," reprinted in *The Philosophy of History in Our Time*, ed. Meyerhoff, p. 213.

should be so, it might be added, the observations of Becker and Beard lose much of their point. For if value judgment is logically ingredient in the very idea of historical inquiry, it would make no sense for historians even to *aspire* to be objective.

The positivist
rejoinder

On the whole, as Hans Meyerhoff has observed, it is philosophers, not historians defending the "scientific" respectability of their disciplines, who have argued most strongly for the possibility of objective history.[8] It is, moreover, largely the same philosophers who support the positivist model of explanation. The connection is not accidental. For the position of these philosophers is roughly as follows. The historian's task, they will say, is to establish facts about the past and to explain them. But if the Hempelian account of explanation is correct, there is no question as to the objectivity of the conclusions historians can draw. For the goal of explanation is to indicate sufficient conditions of what is being explained, and the sufficiency of these conditions will be certified by the fact that explananda will be deducible from them in accordance with empirically validated laws. There is just no room in such investigation for the value judgment of the historian. If there is room for disagreement at all, it could not legitimately have anything to do with the values of the historians concerned. It would be a result of the defectiveness of our knowledge of relevant laws. If, as is generally the case in historical studies, precise or absolutely universal laws are not available, then disagreements about what would count as a sufficient condition may indeed be traceable to differences of *judgment*. But this judgment would not be a *value* judgment; it would be an inductive estimate of probability.

Exactly the same argument will be used regarding the *establishment* of the facts to be explained. The only way to establish a conclusion about the past, it will be claimed, is to argue, in accordance with empirical laws, that the events in question must have occurred. The scientific model outlined by Hempel and others is thus offered as an account of the structure of *verification* as well as of explanation. Once again the notion of an ingredient value judgment is excluded by the very idea of the inquiry. If the values of a historian nevertheless affect the conclusions he draws, we can be sure that something has gone wrong with the conduct of his inquiry.

The opposition to this positivist claim, as in the case of the disagreement over explanation, generally arises out of a certain view of the historian's subject matter—or, what is perhaps inseparable from this, of his way of approaching or conceiving it. Two arguments will be considered here, both of which were used by Beard. The first is that the subject matter of history is itself value charged: a view which has recently been reiterated by such philosophers as Isaiah Berlin and Leo Strauss. The second is that the selection the historian makes in con-

---

[8] *The Philosophy of History in Our Time*, p. 161.

structing a historical account is value guided. The latter, which Mandel-baum calls "the fountain-head of relativism," [9] is an ancient argument, which has often been quickly dismissed. We may find, however, that some important truth lurks in it.

Human actions as value charged   In *Historical Inevitability,* Berlin puts the first argument in the following terms. The historian, he concedes, should certainly avoid "censoriousness." But he can scarcely hope to avoid "that minimal degree of moral or psychological evaluation which is necessarily involved in viewing human beings as creatures with purposes and motives (and not merely as causal factors in the procession of events)." [10] In support of this relativist claim, Berlin points out that history is not a formalized discipline, with a specially devised technical vocabulary. It is an attempt to understand the past in the same terms as those in which the plain man attempts to understand the present in which he has to act.

> We account for the French Revolution, or the character of Napoleon, or the behaviour of Talleyrand, as we would account for the behaviour of our contemporaries . . . with the same rich, scarcely analyzable mixture of physiological and psychological, economic and biographi-cal, aesthetic and ethical, causal and purposive concepts, which pro-vide what we regard as normal and sufficient answers to our normal questions about how and why things or persons act as they do.[11]

In opting to use ordinary language, Berlin contends, the historian is condemned, whether he likes it or not, indeed whether he realizes it or not, to talk evaluatively about his subject matter. For words like "vic-tory," "treason," "order," "statesmanship," which are the common stock of historical description, are not purely descriptive terms.

For those who dislike this way of putting the point—as if it were a matter of the unsuspecting historian falling into a mere linguistic trap—there is another route to virtually the same conclusion, a route taken by Leo Strauss in his *Natural Right and History.*[12] Strauss asks us to con-sider, especially, the history of art and religion. The essential point is that, by including, say, reference to a certain painting in an art history, the historian commits himself to the judgment that it is the genuine article. He judges, for example, that it is not "trash"; and he cannot make such a distinction without appealing to aesthetic standards. Sim-ilarly in religious history: is it possible to write it without making religious judgments—judgments discerning differences of piety or spirit-ual depth, for example? Or history of warfare without assessing the

[9] *The Problem of Historical Knowledge,* p. 20.
[10] Reprinted in part in *The Philosophy of History in Our Time,* ed. Meyerhoff, p. 269.
[11] *Ibid.,* p. 268.
[12] (Chicago: University of Chicago Press, 1953), pp. 50-51, 56-57.

strategy of the generals? More generally, how can the historian write about *anything*, unless he is able to recognize its nature; and how can he grasp such objects of study as these without placing a value upon them?

Now no one is going to deny that we do apply moral, aesthetic, and other kinds of standards in what we ordinarily say about our own and other people's actions. And there is obviously a sense in which these actions "invite" our judgment. Our question, however, is whether we should regard such value judgment as a *necessary* feature of historical inquiry. Ernest Nagel is among those who are sure we should not. He declares:

> It is an obvious blunder to suppose that only a fat cowherd can drive fat kine. It is an equally crude error to maintain that one cannot inquire into the conditions and consequences of values and evaluations without necessarily engaging in moral or aesthetic value-judgments.[13]

Speaking (perhaps with doubtful authority) for professional historians, Herbert Butterfield takes a similar position. Although conceding that "life is a moral matter every inch of the way," Butterfield nevertheless denies that it is the task of the historian, qua historian, to draw moral conclusions. His proper task, he says, is "technical history": a study of "the observable inter-connections of events." To this sort of inquiry, moral judgments are "by their very nature, irrelevant . . ."; they are "alien" to its "intellectual realm." [14]

But relativists are bound to feel that the Nagel-Butterfield rejoinder misses the point. What is at issue, they will say, is not whether a study of "the conditions and consequences" of evaluations can be carried out without *further* evaluations. It is whether what we often wish to investigate further in this way is not itself already *value constituted*, whether the detailed objects of historical study can even be conceived or correctly characterized without an evaluation by the historian. Butterfield's plea for technical history seems completely to disregard this difficulty. He tells us, for example, that "religious persecution" and "military atrocities" are phenomena which the historian should not *judge*, but simply try to understand—as if a judgment were not already implicit in his characterization of the fact. For the objectivists, facts and values are always quite distinct. But if we are to call persecutions and atrocities "facts"—and historians are generally prepared to do so—it is easy to see why evaluation is thought to be logically ingredient in the historian's subject matter.

In the face of such an argument, however, the positivist response may well be to propose a deliberate and "salutary" reform of historical practice. As Mandelbaum has put it, what is valued must surely first

[13] "The Logic of Historical Analysis," *op. cit.*, p. 209.
[14] "Moral Judgment in History" (an extract from *History and Human Relations*), in *The Philosophy of History in Our Time*, ed. Meyerhoff, pp. 229-30.

be known as "object"; we cannot value what we do not (at least think) we know.[15] If this is so, then for every value-charged characterization, or every value-constituted fact, the historian ought to be able to substitute a statement of those features of what occurred, by reference to which he would *defend* his value judgment—a statement which would itself be value free. It may be hard indeed to imagine historians ever carrying out such a reform, even if they could be induced to try. For the incidence of covertly evaluative terms in most historical narratives is a good deal higher than might appear to a casual glance. When G. M. Young refers to the Chartists as "a body of decent, hardly used and not particularly intelligent men," the value judgment is obvious enough. But when G. M. Trevelyan observes that eighteenth century England was "wanting" in public organization—rather than saying, for example, that it was "free" of it—the evaluative implications may more easily be missed. But the question, it might still be argued, is not how cataclysmic the proposed reform would be. It is whether it is compatible with the idea of history that it should be tried.

It has sometimes been suggested that to achieve such an extrusion of value reference, the historian would ultimately be forced to descend to the level of sheer physical description. If this were so, it would be plausible to claim that the proposed reform could be ruled out immediately on logical grounds. For history is a study of human *action*; and, as Collingwood reminds us, a physical event cannot be considered an action in abstraction from the thought which it expresses. The idea of history simply as "a study of human actions" therefore requires that the historian's account should be in thoroughly *purposive* terms. But it is difficult to see how merely attributing a purpose to a historical agent requires the historian's *evaluation* of the action which expresses that purpose.[16] When Berlin concludes that to view men as "creatures with purposes and motives" involves us necessarily in at least "a minimal degree" of moral evaluation, he therefore appears to be mistaken.

It is true that what is sometimes at issue when we ask about the "nature" of an action is, in fact, the appropriateness of a value judgment. A man's action, we may say, was "murder"; that is what he *did*. But we could, of course, deliberately restrict our attention to those aspects of what he did which could be subsumed under the value-neutral term "killing," without ceasing to view the agent as "a creature with purposes and motives." A similar conclusion is warranted in cases where the historian turns from general history to more specialized themes, like

[15] *The Problem of Historical Knowledge*, p. 197. For a more extended discussion, see Ernest Nagel, *The Structure of Science* (New York: Harcourt, Brace & World, Inc., 1961), pp. 488ff.

[16] For a discussion of the thesis that action is nevertheless an "ascriptive," rather than a purely "descriptive," concept, see H. L. A. Hart, "The Ascription of Responsibility and Rights," in *Essays on Logic and Language*, ed. Antony Flew (New York: Philosophical Library, 1951), pp. 160ff Criticisms of this notion may be found in George Pitcher, "Hart on Action and Responsibility," *Philosophical Review*, LXIX, No. 2 (April, 1960), 226-35.

history of politics and war. Even history of art—which others besides Strauss have cited in this connection—is not concerned with value-charged actions in the sense envisaged by the present argument.[17] For artistic trash, if it has artistic intent, is still presumably "art" and thus to be distinguished from other kinds of trash.

The problem of selection   The situation changes, however, if we interpret the distinction between art and trash as reminding us that only *significant* past human actions properly find a place in historical narratives. For this brings us to the second of the relativist arguments mentioned above. This argument is not that the human actions which the historian studies are *in their very nature* value constituted; it is rather that they are necessarily evaluated by the historian in the process of selecting them for a historical account. Beard expresses this second argument thus: "Every written history . . . is a selection and arrangement of facts . . . an act of choice, conviction and interpretation respecting values." [18] What are we to say about the cogency of this?

Two observations may perhaps help to put the argument in perspective. First, we may accept it as *in fact* true that no historian can pack into his narrative all he knows about the object of his inquiry. This will be the case whether he attempts a survey of Western Europe since the fall of Rome or simply tells the story of the crossing of the Rubicon. It is also *in fact* true that when faced with the need to select, the historian generally tells us what he thinks significant or important, and that what he tells us thus has implicit in it a certain standard of value. But although the selectivity of historical accounts might, because of the first consideration, be said to be a necessary *predicament* of historical inquiry, it may appear less obvious that from the second we are justified in concluding that the evaluation of what is known is *required* for the construction of a historical narrative. For it might appear *logically* possible, at least, that a historian should simply select at random. The result, perhaps, would not be very interesting. But it might be argued that it is still *history*.

The rebuttal of this suggestion requires from the relativist a further clarification of the idea of history. He will insist—surely with justification—that a historian who merely juxtaposed true statements about the past, or some object of study in it, would not be constructing a history at all, as we ordinarily understand the word. In this connection, an ambiguity in the word "history," which cuts across the one mentioned in Chapter 1, is of interest. Everything a person does, it may be claimed, whether significant or not, "passes into history." In this sense "history" seems to include the total human past. If a person just carries on in his

---

[17] For a careful and original statement of a contrary view, see Peter Winch, *The Idea of a Social Science and Its Relation to Philosophy*, Studies in Philosophical Psychology (London: Routledge & Kegan Paul, Ltd., 1958), pp. 87ff.

[18] "Written History as an Act of Faith," reprinted in *The Philosophy of History in Our Time*, ed. Meyerhoff, p. 141.

normal, quite unremarkable way, however, he can scarcely claim to be "making history"; and in the same sense, although perhaps with unacceptable quietism, lands have been said to be happier for having had "no history." Here the word is obviously reserved for events and actions which have some importance. Relativists will want to argue that it is history in this second sense which the historian has as his object when he "constructs a history." Doubtless it is less—and dangerously less—than a complete account of the historian's proper function to say, with Jacob Burckhardt, that history is "the record of facts which one age finds remarkable in another." [19] Somewhat better is Jacques Barzun's contention that "exists in history" can be translated "are memorable." [20] What a relativist will deny is that any adequate account can be given of the historian's proper task without some such notion as "memorability." It is interesting to note that, on this point, he would appear to have the Father of History on his side.[21]

The implications for our assessment of the argument from selection would appear to be these. It does not follow logically, from the mere fact that he has to select at all, that the historian imposes standards of value on his material. Insofar as it implies this—as has often been pointed out—the argument from selection is defective. It is rather that if history in the relevant sense is to be written, the historian must select evaluatively because "history" in this sense is a quasi-evaluative notion: the notion not just of the past, but of the significant past. This positive, if still quite vague, criterion of what should be *included* in a history should be distinguished from the point made by Mandelbaum, noted at the beginning of Chapter 2. For in saying that history is confined to human actions of "societal significance," Mandelbaum appears to have meant only that human actions in their purely private aspects could be *excluded*.

If the argument from selection, thus emended, states an important truth about the idea of history, there is something further that might be said about the earlier relativist arguments of Berlin and Strauss. For if the "placing" of each action or event in his narrative requires a judgment of relative importance, it would seem that Strauss is correct in claiming that the historian cannot avoid *regarding* what he describes as value charged. And if this is so, it is surely reasonable to expect the historian's *language* to reflect this, as Berlin says it should. If the reason a certain action warrants a place in the narrative is that it was a murder, rather than a mere killing, it is difficult to see why the historian should deliberately avoid saying so. In spite of its logical possibility, therefore, there is something rather odd about any suggestion that history would be "improved" if the evaluative content of the language of historical description were carefully strained away. To extrude explicit value judg-

[19] Quoted in Karl Löwith, *Meaning in History* (Chicago: University of Chicago Press, 1949; a Phoenix book), p. 20.

[20] "Cultural History: A Synthesis," in *The Varieties of History*, ed. Stern, p. 397.

[21] See, for example, the first sentence of Herodotus' *History*.

ments from the historian's language, at any rate, would not extrude them from his *inquiry*.

Against the position just outlined, objectivists have advanced a number of arguments. One very common one, which threatens to put the whole relativist case immediately out of court, appeals to what some philosophers have called the "principle of nonvacuous contrast." [22] This principle lays it down that "no predicate apply either to everything or to nothing in its universe of discourse." To deny, with point, that an inquiry is objective, we must have in mind a genuine contrast with something to which this epithet could be applied. But this makes it difficult to deny the objectivity of history on the ground that it is selective and evaluative. For the historian's inquiry is not unique in these respects. In some sense, *all* inquiries are selective—including physical science. No scientist can study everything in his field; he must select some aspect or problem, and in doing so, like the historian, he follows his interests and betrays his values. The relativist argument, however, was supposed to show a *difference* between history and science. Since it fails to do so, it labors a "vacuous" contrast.

Now the central claim here—that all inquiry is selective—can hardly be contested. The possibility of rebutting the objection therefore depends upon the relativist's showing that the historian's problem of selection is significantly different from that of the generalizing sciences. In considering this question, there are two distinctions which might well be kept in mind.[23] The first, sometimes recognized but seldom used by the protagonists themselves, is a distinction between selecting a *problem* for study and selecting what is to count as its *solution*, once the problem has been determined. Objectivists often appear to assume that it is selection of the former kind which leads relativists to declare the historian's narrative nonobjective; and it must be conceded that reason is sometimes given for such an assumption. We are told by John Dewey, for example, that all history is "relative to a problem," the problems varying from historian to historian—as if this settled the matter.[24] And certainly it is true that different aspects of what happened seem to raise problems for different people, the asking of different questions indicating a difference of evaluation, if only with respect to what A. O. Lovejoy has called the "extremely important and rather neglected"

[22] See Christopher Blake, "Can History Be Objective?" reprinted in *Theories of History*, ed. Gardiner, p. 332, and a reply by J. A. Passmore, "The Objectivity of History," *Philosophy*, XXXIII, No. 125 (April, 1958), 97ff.

[23] What follows is drawn largely from my "The Historian's Problem of Selection," originally published in *Logic, Methodology and Philosophy of Science*, ed. Ernest Nagel, Patrick Suppes, and Alfred Tarski. Adapted with the permission of the publishers, Stanford University Press. © 1962 by the Board of Trustees of Leland Stanford Junior University.

[24] "Historical Judgments" (an extract from his *Logic: The Theory of Inquiry*), in *The Philosophy of History in Our Time*, ed. Meyerhoff, p. 165.

value of "interestingness." [25] When we ask whether historical *inquiry* is value free, however, our chief concern should not be with this kind of variability. For the different evaluations of historians involved in their decision to ask different questions will be ingredient, not in their *inquiry*, but in their choice of it. It is when historians give different answers to the same questions that the problem of objectivity *within* the inquiry can be said to arise. It is therefore only with respect to the latter that we should seek a contrast with allegedly objective types of inquiry, since they also require the choosing of questions.

A relativist will want to argue, however, that historians *do* give different answers to the same questions; and that, unlike physical scientists, who also, of course, from time to time differ about what answers to give, they do this in circumstances where the difference is attributable to their different value judgments. In this connection it is useful to note a second distinction which might be drawn, this time between two kinds of historical writing. These might be referred to for our purposes as *explanatory* and *descriptive* inquiries. Perhaps the distinction will not be found unambiguously exemplified in any actual histories. But Cecil Woodham-Smith's *The Reason Why* (which gives the background of the Charge of the Light Brigade) and Gibbon's *Decline and Fall of the Roman Empire* may serve as examples of predominantly explanatory histories, while G. M. Young's *Victorian England: Portrait of an Age* or Carlton Hayes' *A Generation of Materialism* (which surveys European history during the last three decades of the nineteenth century) may serve as predominantly descriptive ones. This distinction reflects the view of Harry Elmer Barnes that historians have a dual task: on the one hand, to "trace the genesis of contemporary culture and institutions"; and on the other, to "reconstruct as a totality the civilizations of the leading eras of the past." [26]

The special interest of the distinction for our discussion is to be found in the fact, already noted, that the positivist theory of explanation has often been thought to provide a *general* rebuttal of the argument from selection. With the distinction between explanatory and descriptive history in mind, however, it might be argued that this will not do, *even for those who accept the positivist theory of explanation.* For the problem of selecting answers (rather than questions) in the two sorts of inquiries would appear to be quite different. It may be conceded that, on the positivist theory, the notion of outlining a set of sufficient conditions does offer an *ideal* of objective selection which could conceivably be realized in an explanatory history. There is no corresponding ideal of objective selection for descriptive histories which could conceivably be realized. For the only candidate would appear to be the notion of a

---

[25] "Present Standpoints and Past History," reprinted in *The Philosophy of History in Our Time*, ed. Meyerhoff, pp. 175-76.

[26] *A History of Historical Writing* (Norman: University of Oklahoma Press, 1937), p. 380. Quoted, with disapproval, in J. H. Randall, Jr., *Nature and Historical Experience* (New York: Columbia University Press, 1958), p. 51.

"complete description," and this is something which it is impossible to give. The descriptive historian is, of course, provided by the problem he sets himself with certain nonevaluative criteria of what can be *ruled out*. If he is writing a history of England, for example, there is no problem about whether to select an event which occurred in China in the fourth century B.C. And if he is writing an economic history, he need not consider the claims of, say, a religious revival, except insofar as he considers it a condition of an economic event already selected. But a history is not composed of everything that is left over when such negative criteria have been applied. It is an essential part of the historian's task to determine what shall be *ruled in*. And this is a problem which arises *after* he has selected the subject of his study. The need to select arises *in the course of*, not just *in the choice of*, his inquiry.

Objectivists who would accept what has been said about the way selection presents a problem in descriptive histories may still feel that relativists make too much of it. They will concede, for example, that two historians who set out to write the history of the Reformation—especially if one is a Protestant and the other a Catholic—will produce very different accounts. But this, they will argue, is hardly a basis for such a sharp difference of status between the conclusions of historians and scientists. For if two historians make different selections out of what is known in producing such accounts, there is no need to conclude that either of them writes a *false* account. Nor for that matter need we, strictly speaking, regard them as *contradicting* each other. On the contrary, so long as their different accounts are constructed entirely out of true statements, they will *supplement* each other. It is therefore somewhat misleading even to say that they offer different answers to the same question. Their answers are better regarded as providing "contributions" to the history of the subject in view. And it may plausibly be claimed that this is all any self-respecting historian really hopes to do; he has no foolish ambition to tell "the whole truth" about his subject. To think otherwise, suggests Nagel, is to fall into the idealist "error" of the doctrine of "the internality of all relations": the notion that "one cannot have competent knowledge of anything unless one knows everything." [27]

What makes such a response unsatisfactory to the relativist, in spite of its grain of truth, is the false assumption it seems to make about the nature of the *problem* of a descriptive history. All history may be, as Dewey says, "relative to a problem." But the problem of a descriptive historian writing, say, a history of England, is not correctly formulated as "What are some of the things that happened in England?" It is not even "What are some of the important things?" Historians recognize the legitimacy of a comparison between two differing accounts of the same subject in terms of the "adequacy" of each. One can certainly be judged better than the other; and one can be so bad, without containing any

[27] "The Logic of Historical Analysis," *op. cit.*, p. 209.

false statements, that it will be said no longer to give a "true picture" at all. What, for example, should we think of a one-volume "portrait" of Victorian England that ignored the working class movement? Or a history of Nazi Germany which failed to mention the mass murder of the Jews? Such omissions would always require to be defended on the ground that—the specification of the subject of the inquiry being what it was—what *was* included was *more* important. There is an ideal which is properly operative in every descriptive history, for which the "non-competitive" theory seems to leave little scope. Morton White, in an interesting search for objective criteria (short of "full description") in this connection, suggests that a historian, within his self-imposed limits of scale and subject matter, aims at giving what he conceives to be the "deepest" or most "representative" truths. But he concedes that these latter notions cannot be analyzed nonevaluatively;[28] they are just concealed ways of referring to judgments of importance.

Instrumental and intrinsic importance

This brings us to a further, and perhaps the most characteristic, objection to the relativist thesis. In raising it, the objectivist concedes that the historian may be criticized for having failed to select what was really important. But "importance," even in descriptive histories, he will argue, is a *causal* notion; it is not to be elucidated in terms of the value scheme of the historian. What warrants the inclusion of an item in the narrative, as White once put it, is its "causal fertility."[29] Dewey appears also to have a causal criterion in mind when he writes: "There is no history except in terms of movement toward some outcome. . . . The selection of outcome . . . determines the selection and organization of subject-matter."[30] In considering this objection, we shall not here question what appears to be the assumption that causal judgment is itself value free. (This is a question to which we shall return in Chapter 4.) We shall ask only whether it can be claimed that causal importance is *the* criterion of selection in descriptive history.

Now it is obvious that very often it is. Events often properly find a place in the historian's narrative because of their importance *for other things*; they are judged to be important because of what they lead to. But to say that this *must* be the principle of selection in a history that sets out to describe, squares neither with the notion of description, nor with our expectations of historians, nor with their own normal practice. In a history of Victorian England, for example, the working-class movement may indeed be referred to because of its influence, say, on the

[28] "The Logic of Historical Narration," in *Philosophy and History*, ed. Hook. pp. 11ff. For a somewhat more objectivist argument see his "Can History Be Objective?" reprinted in *The Philosophy of History in Our Time*, ed. Meyerhoff, p. 195.

[29] "Toward an Analytic Philosophy of History," in *Philosophic Thought in France and the United States*, ed. Marvin Farber (Buffalo, N. Y.: University of Buffalo Publications in Philosophy, 1950), p. 719.

[30] "Historical Judgments," *op. cit.*, p. 171. For similar language, see Randall, *Nature and Historical Experience*, p. 43.

political transition from liberalism to socialism. But it may equally well warrant a place in the story because it shows what human beings, challenged by the social chaos of industrialism, can do; and as such it may be judged *intrinsically* interesting. To leave it out would present a distorted account of Victorian England. Similarly, reference to the mass murder of Jews may be selected because of its bearing on the functioning of the upper echelons of the Nazi party and government. But even if it were not, it would have a claim to be mentioned because of its intrinsic importance as a monument of human depravity. All selection may be "relative to a problem," but the problem in descriptive history, at least in part, is to find out what is *worth* noticing. And what makes an event worth noticing does not *have* to be its tendency to produce something else.[31]

It might be remarked in this connection that even where an event or action described can hardly claim by itself to be intrinsically important, the criterion which warrants its inclusion will not necessarily be a *causal* one—at any rate, not in the straightforward way considered so far. "More immediately significant than the growth of population," writes G. M. Young of early Victorian England, "was its aggregation in great towns."[32] What kind of significance is this? Not causal, surely; for Young's point is not that this aggregation led to something else. The significance lies rather in the fact that the concentration of population was *part* of a new pattern of life which Young is trying to depict and characterize. It is significant, no doubt, in relation to something else— but that something is the whole social complex which is being contrasted here with what is referred to as an earlier "rural and patrician" way of life.[33]

Against this, it may still perhaps be objected that even if the criterion in such a case is not a causal one, it is clearly not evaluative either. The reason Young brings in the part—the population concentration—is that he is talking about the whole—the industrialization of England, or something of the kind. It may further be argued that what is said to be mentioned because of its *intrinsic* importance—the industrialization—is itself nonevaluatively determined by the *subject* of the inquiry—Victorian England, or perhaps certain selected aspects of it. Such an objection, if valid, would be very damaging for the relativist case as it has been presented here. For what it does, in effect, is transfer the historian's evaluation from the point at which he selects an *answer* to the question "What was Victorian England like?" to the point at which he selects *questions* to ask about the object of his inquiry, Vic-

[31] W. H. Walsh presents a strong argument of this kind in "The Limits of Scientific History," in *Historical Studies III*, ed. James Hogan (New York: Hillary House, Inc., 1961), pp. 45-57.

[32] *Victorian England: Portrait of an Age*, 2nd ed. (New York: Oxford University Press, 1953), p. 21.

[33] Mandelbaum recognizes such noncausal "linkage" between historical events in "Objectivity in History," in *Philosophy and History*, ed. Hook, p. 46.

torian England. And the latter would involve only a kind of value judgment which we have already agreed to disregard, since it is common to all inquiry.

In considering this objection, a further distinction might be drawn between kinds of histories, this time within the descriptive class. This is a distinction between what might be called "theme" and "period" histories. Typical of the former is G. M. Trevelyan's *The English Revolution*. Typical of the latter are the descriptive histories by Young and Hayes which have already been mentioned. The basis of the distinction is that a theme history has a subject determined by the sort of unity which makes us call it a single event, movement, state of affairs, etc., whereas the subject of a period history is determined chiefly by spatio-temporal criteria. The limiting case of period history is universal history. It is sometimes objected that it is impossible to inquire about history-as-a-whole, on the ground that history is not a whole.[34] But this is to assume that only theme histories are legitimate. To assert the possibility of a study of history-as-a-whole does not imply that history *is* a whole of some kind apart from being history-as-a-whole. The assertion that history is a whole—which amounts to the assertion that all historical events of a certain scale of intrinsic importance form a single pattern, whether causal, purposive, or dramatic—is either an unlikely empirical hypothesis, or a dubious a priori thesis, of certain speculative philosophers of history, some of whose constructions we are later to examine. The writing of universal history of the period type, on the other hand, seems to face no problem except that of finding out enough to make it worth attempting.

Whatever we say about universal history, it seems clear that Young's history is of the period type; its subject is defined by reference to the reign of Queen Victoria. It is quite possible, of course, that Young decided to write his history because he saw some kind of unity in the period. But having selected this subject, he is bound to convey to us only as much of this unity as a balanced "portrait" of the period warrants. The point is even clearer in the case of Hayes. For in his case, the very title of his book, *A Generation of Materialism*, may arouse the expectation that his history will have a thematic unity, as the exploration of the manifestations of a certain frame of mind or outlook. To think, however, that Hayes begins with the *topic*, "The Materialistic Generation of the Nineteenth Century," is to get the logical force of what he is telling us all wrong. "A Generation of Materialism" is not the specification of the subject of his inquiry; it is his considered description-cum-

[34] E.g., Randall, *Nature and Historical Experience*, p. 39. For good statements, by historians, of the view that all history requires the concept of "universal history," see Henri Pirenne, "What Are Historians Trying to Do?" reprinted in *The Philosophy of History in Our Time*, ed. Meyerhoff, p. 88, and Geoffrey Barraclough, "Universal History," reprinted in *Approaches to History*, ed. H. P. R. Finberg (Toronto: University of Toronto Press, 1962), pp. 83-110.

assessment of it. He does not begin by setting himself the problem of describing something which stands out as a social unity. He begins, rather, by *looking* for unity in his period. If he had not found it, or had found many such themes, he would not in any sense have lost his grip on his subject—although he might then have had to call his book simply *Europe in the Late Nineteenth Century*. This interpretation, incidentally, finds an echo in his editor's instruction: to make clear, within the prescribed decades, "the main movements in European history." [35]

Now if it is allowed that the selection of "main movements," the criteria for which are not supplied by the specification of the subject of the inquiry, involves the historian's use of value judgment, and if it is allowed that it is legitimate to attempt the construction of histories of the period type at all, then the relativist case is surely a strong one. Perhaps few would deny the first of these contentions. The second is, admittedly, sometimes brought into question. It seems to be on the ground, for example, that a projected "History of England" would have no unity of theme, and would thus be what we have called a period history in disguise, that John Passmore tells us "there is no such subject as *The History of England*." This, he says, is a "preposterous" title for a book. [36] J. H. Randall, Jr. has expressed similar views. The response of the relativist, however, would surely be that any theory of history which results in the ruling out of such constructions is a preposterous theory of history. It seems to abandon, at any rate, the attempt to elucidate the idea of history historians actually have. And if it owes any of its attractiveness to the belief that theme histories, at least, can be constructed without *any* judgments of intrinsic importance, it seems to rest upon an illusion. For a historian of the French Revolution, for example, can scarcely determine what to include, nonevaluatively, from the fact that the event he studies is a revolution and French and began in 1789.

Past and present values Some of those who would accept, in general, the notion that standards of intrinsic importance must enter into historical reconstruction of the past have gone on to raise a further question, one which may be thought to reopen the whole problem of objectivity in a new way. This is the question whether, strictly speaking, it is the historian's *own* values—or even those of his audience or society—which must or should guide the selection of what is important. For it has been argued by some theorists that the operative values, if a historian wants to approach the past in a properly "historical" way, should be those of the period which he has in view. This position has been elegantly expressed by A. O. Lovejoy in an attack on what he takes to be John

[35] Hayes, *A Generation of Materialism* (New York: Harper & Row, Publishers, 1941), p. x.
[36] "The Objectivity of History," *op. cit.*, pp. 103-4.

Dewey's overly pragmatic view of history.[37] The arguments on either side are as follows.

For Dewey, "everything in the writing of history depends upon the principle used to control selection." That principle in turn depends, he tells us, on the interests and perplexities of the historian himself, so that "all history is necessarily written from the standpoint of the present"; it is the history of "that which is contemporaneously judged to be important in the present." There are two possible interpretations of this, however, which it is vital to distinguish. As we have already found relativists arguing, it may simply be taken to mean that it is standards of importance or value current in the historian's own "present" that determine what is worthy of selection. Lovejoy, however, interprets Dewey's dictum much more strongly as the claim that all history must be "instrumental to the settlement of a present [theoretical] problem or the determination of a present program of action." And the illustrations Dewey offers of his thesis do, at any rate, suggest such an interpretation. Thus he writes: "The urgency of the social problems which are now developing out of the forces of industrial production and distribution, is the source of a new interest in history from the economic point of view." And again: "When current problems seem dominantly political, the political aspect of history is uppermost." For Lovejoy, this represents a serious confusion of the approach of the historian with that of the philosopher or social reformer; it represents the very antithesis of "historical mindedness." What Dewey describes is not history itself, but a certain *use* to which historical conclusions may be put. Lovejoy does not, of course, deny that they can ever have such a use. What he denies is that usefulness for solving present problems affords a proper criterion for selection in what purports to be "the history" of an age, movement, or institution.

What, then, is the alternative? Lovejoy's account of historical mindedness is worth quoting:

> To study history is always to seek in some degree to get beyond the limitations and preoccupations of the present; it demands for success an effort of self-transcendence. It is not impossible nor unprofitable for a rational animal—and it is imperative for the historian—to realize that his ancestors had ends of their own which were not solely instrumental to his ends, that the content and meaning of their existence are not exhaustively resolvable into those of the existence of their posterity. In these aspects of history lie not the least of its values; for it is they, especially, which make of it a mind-enlarging, liberalizing, sympathy-widening discipline, an enrichment of present experience.[38]

When a historian gives an account of a past period or society, therefore, "the selection should be determined, not by what seems important to

---

[37] Lovejoy, "Present Standpoints" and Dewey, "Historical Judgments," *op. cit.*, pp. 163-87.
[38] "Present Standpoints," *op. cit.*, p. 181.

him, but by what seemed important to other men." This is what "differentiates historical from any other type of relevance and significance."

Now the position Lovejoy here outlines is a valuable corrective to any crudely pragmatic theory of history. It is of special interest for our discussion because it would reinforce the objectivist argument presented earlier (and attributed to Nagel) that, although the historian is concerned with values, these values are *given* by his subject matter; they are "historical facts" like any others. One may doubt, however, whether Lovejoy's own account of historical significance is acceptable without serious qualification. Where he is on strong ground is in insisting that the idea of history is the idea of a study of the past *for its own sake*. Its object, as Oakeshott has put it (perhaps more mysteriously), is not the "practical past." [39] We should be careful, however, not to confuse this thesis with the distinguishable and further claim that the past should be studied exclusively *in its own terms*. Idealist philosophers of history constantly remind us that history is an attempt to recreate a past form of life; that this requires the historian (and his reader) to get "inside" that form of life, to "re-think" its thoughts, and perhaps to re-experience at least an echo of its hopes and fears. And they are surely right to say that at least a part of the historian's task is consequently to understand past ages "as they understood themselves"—this requiring us to take on, for the purpose of understanding, *their* standards of what was important. What is doubtful is that this is *all* the historian is expected to do.

Historians themselves sometimes display uncertainty about this when they theorize about their inquiry. In *History in a Changing World*, Geoffrey Barraclough finds much that is "salutary and true" in the view that, in historical study, "we should judge past ages—if we judge them at all—by their own standards, and not by ours"; that we should "give importance to what was important then, and not single out, in earlier centuries, only those phases and incidents which seem of importance to us." [40] On reflection, however, he recoils from the consequences of this view. If we followed the judgment of those who bothered to write on thirteenth century England, he points out, we should produce "a dreary recital of miracles, tempests, comets, pestilences, calamities and other 'wonderful things.'" The historian, he concludes, should be concerned, "not with what was important, but with what *we think* was (or ought to have been) important."

The most empathetic historians, it seems, stand back from time to time to give an *estimate* of what they have discovered in terms of standards their own period did not necessarily share. The critical comparison of different ages presupposes the legitimacy of such evaluation.

---

[39] *Experience and Its Modes*, pp. 103ff. For a direct denial of this, see Becker's claim that in the historical study of Magna Carta "we are interested in it for our own sake, and not for its sake." "What Are Historical Facts?" *op. cit.*, p. 121.

[40] (Norman: University of Oklahoma Press, 1956), pp. 21-22.

So do such judgments as the following, made by Max Beloff in *The Age of Absolutism:*

> But Portugal itself with its 2,000,000 inhabitants no longer possessed the élan that had made its history in the fifteenth and sixteenth centuries so full of enterprise and adventure; it was in 1660 despite the growing wealth of Brazil a Power quite clearly of secondary rank.[41]

Beloff does not mean that this was clear to the Portuguese; he does not even mean that it was clear to her enemies. He is telling us not how things *seemed* to the protagonists, but how (in *his* judgment) they actually *were*. In the following comment on the last quarter of the nineteenth century, W. L. Langer employs the latter distinction explicitly.

> It was an era of peace in Europe, an age of great technological advance, a period of progress, of growing tolerance, of spreading liberalism. Or so at least it seemed at the time and so it appears to many even now. And yet, when viewed historically, when examined critically, the late nineteenth century emerges rather as an age of materialism, of smug self-confidence, or uncritical assurance.[42]

Historians like C. V. Wedgwood, who concentrate largely on showing us how things appeared to the participants, it might be noted, are seldom regarded by their fellows as attaining the highest rank. They seem to be regarded, indeed, in much the same way that theoretical scientists regard those in *their* field who do not go beyond the level of classification and empirical generalization. In both cases, although in different ways, the idea of the inquiry requires a further interpretation of the materials thus provided. Historical inquiry might thus be said to employ two standpoints: it seeks to understand past ages as far as possible in their own terms, but it does this preparatory to judging them in broader terms. Since the standards employed at the second level will be those which the historian believes *in the present* to be valid, it might be said that present values *ought* to enter historical reconstruction.

The question remains, however, whether it is really possible to extrude such value judgments, even at the first level of inquiry. The question is of importance, since to allow that the past *might* be reconstructed entirely in terms of its own standards of importance may seem to offer a basis for a reformulated objectivism. Leo Strauss, for example, sometimes appears inclined to divide the responsibilities of discovering the appearances and the realities of the past between the historians and social scientists respectively, with historical reconstruction employing only the values of the participants.[43] The reply of the relativist, however, is usually this. The study of the past from a standpoint into which the historian's own values do not enter is surely possible only "to a degree." For *whose* values represent *the* values of the period in question?

---

[41] (New York: Hillary House, Inc., 1954), p. 34.
[42] Hayes, *A Generation of Materialism*, p. x.
[43] *Natural Right and History*, p. 57.

In writing the history of the Roman invasion of Britain, do we adopt the standards of the Romans or the Britons? In writing the history of the Protestant Reformation, those of the Catholics or the Protestants? To refer to "the" standards of a past age, it will be argued, is in part to judge *whose* views in that age really mattered. Perhaps this is the correct residue of Dewey's claim that all history is *necessarily* written from the standpoint of the present.[44]

Objective histories   Before concluding this chapter, there are two points on which it might be wise to make a remark or two. The first concerns the limitation which has been deliberately imposed on the sense of the term "objective." Throughout our discussion, we have interpreted the notion of an "objective" history as equivalent to a history which is "value free"; and, as we have seen, the term is in fact often used this way, not only by philosophers, but by historians themselves. It is important to add, however, that historians seem to use it so chiefly in their philosophical, "off-duty" discussions of the general nature of their inquiry. In "on duty" talk *between* historians, it seldom, if ever, carries such a sense.

This fact has been made the basis of some recent discussions of the question "Is history objective?" by so-called "ordinary language" philosophers. According to Christopher Blake, for example, this is really a rather silly question.[45] For the answer is obvious: some histories are and some are not—the same sort of answer we should have to give to a question like "Are stories interesting?" What we should ask rather is "What *makes* a history objective?" or "What kind of objectivity can we *expect* from a historian?" To the latter question, Blake replies: Exactly the kind that an Englishman would attribute to the *Times*, by contrast with the *Mirror*. Yet the difference is difficult to put into words without employing near synonyms like "unbiased" or "lacking tendentiousness." As we ordinarily use the word, "objective" does not mean the same as "true"; it does not even just mean "respectful of the truth," although this is part of it. To apply the term to a report, Blake says, is to imply that "any reasonable person would accept it." The latter is probably too strong; for a piece of work can be *known* to be both objective and wrong. Perhaps two of the chief features, in historical cases, are absence of what Berlin called "censoriousness": an emphasis on value judgment beyond what is required simply to "place" component items in a historical narrative; and an absence of a certain ulterior "interest": in part, what transmutes history into propaganda. What it does *not* mean is that the work contains no value judgments, or even no such judgments with which the speaker disagrees. A Roman Catholic could quite consistently

---

[44] Two ways have been noted above in which history might be said to be relative to the present. *Both* should be distinguished from still a third: that history is relative to the present in the sense that it *explains* it, and that the criterion of selection is the extent to which an event contributed to bringing it about. This view seems to be at least hinted at by Dewey.

[45] "Can History Be Objective?" *op. cit.*, pp. 330ff.

say that a certain Protestant historian's work was objective, while re-fusing to stand committed to all the values expressed in it. Max Fisch sums it up like this:

> The historian is not blamed for praising and blaming, and praised for doing neither, but blamed if antecedent judgments of value blind him to contrary evidence, and praised if his selection and treatment of evidence is clearly not unbalanced by the desire to support judgments formed in advance of the search for evidence. . . . The historian of art is a critic of art, the historian of science a critic of science, and similarly the historian of economic, social and political institutions is a critic of those institutions. Objectivity is not absence of criticism, but unre-served submission to further criticism, complete openness, withholding nothing from judgment.[46]

In drawing attention to the ordinary historical use of "objective," Blake's point, as he remarks himself, represents an application of the principle of nonvacuous contrast. The application differs, however, from the one noted earlier in this chapter. For the possibility of genu-ine contrast which is said to be required in this case is one within the class, not of *inquiries*, but of *histories*. Passmore rightly criticizes Blake for seeming to imply that his principle shows the question "Is history (all of it) objective?" to be without sense or point.[47] For, as we have seen, the implicit contrast here can be with other types of inquiries, such as science.[48] And that, of course, is the way it has been taken in our discussion.

A comment is perhaps required on still a second point. In using freedom from value judgment as a criterion of objectivity, it may seem that we have taken sides on the question whether value judgments are themselves objective. This was not intended. It is in fact true that most of those who have been *concerned* about the role of such judgments in historical inquiry have tended to assume that there is no rational way of reaching agreement on such matters; and denying that value judg-ments themselves, on this broader criterion, were "objective," they have consequently denied the "encomium" (as Blake calls it) to a value-charged history as well. The position taken on this issue, however, clearly need not affect the main focus of our discussion here. That centered on the question whether historical inquiry in concept or idea is value free, in the sense that science is assumed to be. And this question about the "logic" of historical inquiry remains equally for a person who regards value judgments themselves as objective in the sense of being decidable by reason.

[46] "The Philosophy of History: A Dialogue," *Philosophy* (Tokyo), (1959), p. 167.
[47] "The Objectivity of History," *op. cit.*, p. 97.
[48] That science is value free has also recently been questioned. See Richard Rudner, "The Scientist *Qua* Scientist Makes Value Judgments," *Philosophy of Science*, XX, No. 1 (January, 1953), 1-6; R. C. Jeffrey, "Valuation and Acceptance of Scientific Hypotheses," *Philosophy of Science*, XXIII, No. 3 (July, 1956), 237-46; and Issac Levi, "Must the Scientist Make Value Judgments?" *Journal of Philosophy*, LVII, No. 11 (May, 1960), 345-56.

CAUSAL JUDGMENT

IN HISTORY

4

Problems
about causes
In the two preceding chapters we have discussed certain philosophical issues which arise out of the concepts of historical understanding and historical objectivity. It may be useful to conclude
this brief introduction to philosophy of history on its critical side by
going on to a problem which, in the view of some philosophers brings
together in an even more troublesome and compelling way some of the
issues already considered. This is the problem of the nature, meaning,
status, and even legitimacy of the specifically causal judgments historians
make in the conduct of their inquiries.

Few theoretical questions about their discipline seem to have
bothered historians more than this one. There is, as Mandelbaum has
observed, a widespread "distrust" of causal judgment in history.[1] On the
part of some, this is due to what they regard as the extreme difficulty of
making warrantable causal judgments. In the Introduction to his *Causes
of the Civil War*, Kenneth Stampp declares: "As one reflects upon the
problem of causation, it becomes perfectly evident that historians will
never know, objectively and with mathematical precision, what caused
the Civil War. Working with fragmentary evidence, possessing less
than a perfect understanding of human behavior, and finding it impossible to isolate one historical factor to test its significance apart from
all others, historians must necessarily be somewhat tentative and
diffident in drawing their conclusions."[2] By others, however, the problem seems to be located less in the difficulty of the inquiry than in the
concept of causation itself. Most historians, according to Crane Brinton,

---

[1] "Causal Analysis in History," *Journal of the History of Ideas*, III, No. 1
(January, 1942), 30.
[2] (Englewood Cliffs, N. J.: Prentice-Hall, Inc., 1959), p. vi.

would reject the notion of "cause" as an "oversimplification." [3] Charles Beard objects that its application involves "an arbitrary delimitation in time and space." [4] For G. J. Renier, causation is a "postulate," which may easily encourage the "superstitious belief" that historical events are predictable.[5] And a group of American historians, a few years ago, agreed that "cause" was "an ambiguous term of varied and complex meaning"—"a convenient figure of speech, describing motives, influences, forces, and other antecedent interrelations not fully understood." [6]

Those who accept the positivist theory of explanation will find little excuse for such a chorus of alarm and dismay. They will agree with M. R. Cohen that "in its most rigorous form, causality denotes the sum of necessary and sufficient conditions for the occurrence of any event." [7] And the positivist theory makes clear how such necessity and sufficiency are to be certified. If historians are often unable to discover the complete set of such conditions, the conceptual moral is clear. Either they can refer to the conditions they do discover as a "part" of the cause of what occurred, or they can refer to them as *the* cause—in which case they will not, of course, be applying the concept "in its most rigorous form." Whichever they do, once the distinction between a rigorous and loose usage has been understood, there is no further *conceptual* puzzle to be solved about "the nature of the historian's causal judgment." There is only the workaday *historical* problem of identifying at least a few of the conditions without which the effect would not have occurred.

But to write off as simply a matter of "loose usage" all deviations from the ideal of causal judgment thus outlined is not a very plausible procedure. It can hardly be claimed, for example, that when historians limit themselves, as they normally do in making causal judgments, to mentioning only one or a few conditions of what occurred, they do this because they do not know what the rest of them are. It is quite obvious that they often *do* know of at least some other such conditions, but that these are *consciously* excluded (perhaps as mere "background conditions") when the causal judgment is made. The historian of the World War II, for example, may agree that the good health of Winston Churchill was one of the conditions necessary for the rallying of the British nation in 1940; but he will scarcely list this as a cause of it. And historians of the American Civil War have been arguing for over a century as to which of a number of conditions, most of them agreed to be relevant to the outbreak, was actually its *cause*. Some relevant conditions, in other words, appear to be more likely candidates for causal status than others; and the fact of serious controversy raises the

---

[3] Review, *Journal of the History of Ideas*, III, No. 2 (April, 1942), 231.

[4] *Theory and Practice in Historical Study*, Social Science Research Council Bulletin 54 (New York: The Council, 1946), p. 136, n. 3.

[5] *History: Its Purpose and Method* (Boston: Beacon Press, Inc., 1950), p. 181.

[6] *Theory and Practice in Historical Study*, pp. 136-37.

[7] "Causation and Its Application to History," *Journal of the History of Ideas*, III, No. 1 (January, 1942), 19.

question whether some *principle* may not be at work behind the tendency to discriminate between causal and noncausal conditions.

Objection may also be taken to the view expressed above as to the *connection* a cause, once selected, must have with its effect. On the positivist theory, it will be argued that, even if what is selected as cause is not *itself* a sufficient condition of its effect, in claiming that it *was* the cause, we implicitly claim that it completes a (perhaps unspecified) sufficient set of such conditions: we claim, in other words, that the circumstances being what they were, the occurrence of the cause made the occurrence of the effect inevitable. In this sense at least, there is a *necessary connection* between cause and effect. But historians are seldom willing to stand committed to this kind of claim about the events they study. The belief that it may nevertheless be implied by the language of cause and effect sometimes moves them, in fact, to deny that it is proper for historians to make causal judgments at all. The most a historian can do, declares Jacques Barzun, in defending the conception of history as a liberal art, is to "describe conditions." [8] The passage earlier quoted from R. G. Collingwood's *The Idea of History* may appear to lend the support of idealist philosophy to the same conclusion. For Collingwood there contrasts the historian's search for "understanding" with the *further* concern of the natural scientist to discover causes by assigning events to classes between which general (i.e., necessary) relations can be discovered. Yet the use of causal language by historians is obviously widespread. And it is difficult to believe that this is simply a mistake: that the historian's causal judgments cannot mean what they say.

Causes and reasons   A closer look at Collingwood, in fact, shows that this was not his own position. He did not deny that historians properly make causal judgments. What he claimed was that they use the term "cause" in a special sense.[9] A specifically historical sense is needed, according to him, because *what* is caused in history are not natural events, but the actions of "conscious and responsible" agents—or what is reducible to these. Causing a man to act, in this sense, "means affording him a motive for doing it." Depending on the motive involved, we may also speak in such cases of the agent being "made," "induced," "persuaded," or "compelled" to act. An example would be: "Mr. Baldwin's speech caused the adjournment of the House." "In the same sense," Collingwood adds, "we may say that a solicitor's letter causes a man to pay a debt or that bad weather causes him to return from an expedition." It may seem a bit startling to find that it was an essential part of Collingwood's doctrine that what is caused in the present sense is al-

---

[8] "History as a Liberal Art," *Journal of the History of Ideas*, VI, No. 1 (January, 1945), 86-87.

[9] The point is mentioned in *The Idea of History*, p. 214; but the account given below is derived from his more extended discussion in *An Essay on Metaphysics* (New York: Oxford University Press, 1940), pp. 290-95.

ways a *free* act. Since we are told, at the same time, that the causes in question can *compel* or *make* the agent act the way he does—indeed this turns out to be an essential feature—it is evident that the sense of freedom which Collingwood takes to be so closely bound up with the historian's sense of "cause" cannot be freedom by contrast with co-ercion. It must be "freedom of the will" in its traditional philosophical sense: a sense which denies that actions have "sufficient conditions" in antecedent events.

There is obviously a connection between Collingwood's present doctrine and the account he gave of explanations in terms of the "thought" of the historical agent. The explanation of actions is provided by reference to the agent's reason for acting. Collingwood now points out that such reasons can be causes in a special sense. Having been given by Baldwin's speech a reason for adjourning the House, the Speaker therefore adjourned it. If questioned later as to what *caused* him to do this, what he will try to make us see is the way the speech provided him with a very pressing reason for adjourning. The "force" of causes in this sense might therefore be said to be a *rational* one. It is through the agent's recognition of the claim, in reason, which they make upon him to act, that they achieve what we call their effects. It follows that a "cause," in the historical sense, might have failed to have an effect. For to be effective, the agent has to *accept* it as his cause, to *make* it his cause. To put it another way: if an agent has cause to act, and acts accordingly, then what gave him cause to act may become a historical cause of his action. But we cannot, in advance, rule out the possibility that he will fail to act accordingly.

For Collingwood, then, a cause, if it is to be called a necessary condition of an action in history, is necessary not in the sense that without it the action *could not* have been performed: it is necessary only in the sense that without it there would not have been good reason to perform it. Similarly, if a cause is to be called a sufficient condition, it is to be called so, not in the sense that, given it, the action would necessarily be performed, but only in the sense that it renders the course of action in question "rationally required." To this it might be added that, since causes are conceived as "forcing" people to act, only what offers sufficient reason for doing what the agent otherwise does not *want* to do will count as causes in the rational, historical sense; for only these can properly be said to "make," "induce," or "compel." Be-cause they are *causes*, they must inhibit the agent's freedom. But because they are causes of *actions*, they cannot, for Collingwood, be con-nected with their effects in the law-instantiating way; for this would cancel the "free will" of the agent.

The relativity
of causes   Collingwood's notion of a special historical sense of "cause" offers an account of the *connection* between cause and effect quite dif-ferent from that of the positivist theory. He also has some inter-esting things to say about the *contrast* often drawn between causes and

other relevant conditions. Unfortunately, he discusses the latter question with reference only to the causal judgments we make in what he calls "practical science," and in everyday attempts to deal with our physical environment. We shall therefore look briefly first at what he says about this special range of cases,[10] and then ask what, if any, are its implications for the analysis of causal judgment in history.

According to Collingwood, our ordinary idea of a cause is the idea of a "handle" by means of which we can manipulate our environment. The term thus "expresses an idea relative to human conduct": it is "anthropocentric." To refer to one of his illustrations:

> If my car fails to climb a steep hill, and I wonder why, I shall not consider my problem solved by a passer-by who tells me that the top of the hill is further away from the earth's centre than its bottom, and that consequently more power is needed to take a car uphill than to take her along the level.

This is true, but not a proper answer. What I expect, if I want to know the cause of the stoppage, is more like the diagnosis of a mechanic, who "opens the bonnet, holds up a loose high-tension lead, and says: 'look here, sir, you're running on three cylinders.'" The latter condition—no more "necessary" than the former—is the cause because it is a condition which I can correct. Collingwood adds:

> If I had been a person who could flatten out hills by stamping on them, the passer by would have been right to call my attention to the hill as the cause of the stoppage; not because the hill was a hill, but because I was able to flatten it out.

From this kind of analysis, Collingwood derives what he calls the principle of the *relativity of causes*. This may be stated: "for any given person, the cause . . . of a given thing is that one of its conditions which he is able to produce or prevent." Very significant conclusions for *disagreements* about causes follow from this. Suppose, Collingwood says, that

> a car skids while cornering at a certain point, strikes the kerb and turns turtle. From the car-driver's point of view the cause of the accident was cornering too fast, and the lesson is that one must drive more carefully. From the county surveyor's point of view the cause was a defect in the surface or camber of the road, and the lesson is that greater care must be taken to make roads skid-proof. From the motor-manufacturer's point of view the cause was defective design in the car, and the lesson is that one must place the centre of gravity lower.

If this is so, we must say that causal judgments are not just, in general, relative to human concerns—they are in each case relative to one or other of many possible specific "standpoints." It follows that disagreements between those who make such judgments from *different* standpoints may often be traceable to arguing at cross-purposes.

[10] *An Essay on Metaphysics*, pp. 296-312.

Collingwood himself is willing to push this analysis to the point of claiming that in abstraction from a standpoint involving a specific practical concern on the part of the one making the judgment, the notion of a cause makes no sense. "For a mere spectator," he says, "there are no causes." Some of the sting is removed from this, perhaps, by the proviso that he is talking only about the meaning the term bears in "practical science" and its everyday equivalents. But even if we cannot, without qualification, generalize Collingwood's doctrine, he does seem to be right to insist that in the range of contexts he considers, causal judgment makes a *dual* assertion. It certifies something as one of the necessary conditions of what occurred. But it *also* contrasts this condition with other necessary conditions as having some special importance for a person at a certain standpoint. We must ask whether something analogous to this is not true also of causal judgments in history.

Now clearly there are reasons why the doctrine of the relativity of causes, as it has just been stated, cannot apply directly to historical cases. For a historian cannot sensibly ask himself how *he* could have produced or prevented the defeat of Napoleon or the outbreak of the Civil War. In view of what Collingwood says about the way we are to conceive the causes of rational action, it is doubtful, furthermore, that the standpoint of "manipulability," even if we have in mind the powers and opportunities of some person living at the time, is an appropriate one for historical inquiry. For Collingwood makes it clear that a causal judgment in the sense elucidated by the criterion of the "handle" is a deterministic one: it assumes that the condition selected as cause completes a set of conditions jointly sufficient for the occurrence under study; and we have already found him repudiating such an assumption in the case of rational causes in history. Yet where a reason for acting is cited as cause by a historian, what is mentioned is seldom by itself the agent's full "case" for doing what he did. The fact that Mr. Baldwin said what he did would not, presumably, have provided a rational cause for the adjournment of the House, had the Speaker not taken many other aspects of his situation into account. In this sort of example too, there are *many* conditions relevant to the complete (rational) explanation of what was done, even if these do not form a sufficient set in the positivist sense. Thus even if Collingwood is right about the difference between causal assertions in practical science and in history, he is left with the problem of their similarity: *both* discriminate between conditions, all of which are relevant (in an appropriate way) to what is called the effect. We may therefore expect in historical cases another manifestation of the principle of the relativity of causes.

A hint as to what we may possibly find in such cases may perhaps be derived from Collingwood's account of the origins of the concept of historical causation. " '*Causa*,' " he points out, "originally meant 'guilt,' 'blame' or 'accusation,' and when first it began to mean 'cause,' which it sometimes does in fifth-century literature, it was used [in its historical sense] for the cause of a war or the like." We are all, of course, familiar with the fact that causal diagnosis is often carried out in contexts in which the chief interest of the investigation is in the assigning of responsibility or blame. It is vital to see, however, that the hypothesis suggested by Collingwood's remarks turns upside down the usual notion of the relation between finding the cause of something done and assigning blame for it. For it would normally be said that we would have to discover first whose action was the cause before we could say who was to blame. What is being suggested here is rather that it may be necessary, at least in some contexts of investigation, to determine first who (of all those whose actions may count as necessary conditions of what occurred) was to blame. This prior conclusion then affords a principle of selection for determining whose action was the cause. If this is so, it should be noted, the causal conclusion drawn is itself a quasi-evaluative one. This suggests that those considerations discussed in Chapter 3, which have often been used by relativists to deny the "objectivity" of descriptive history, may apply to at least some kinds of explanatory histories as well.

A historical example   Whether historians characteristically use such a principle can be adequately determined only by conducting a survey of reputable historical practice. It may therefore be of interest to look in a little detail at the varying causal judgments which historians have actually made about some widely studied event. Remembering Stampp's remarks, we may select for examination some main lines of development in the causal historiography of the American Civil War.[11] Since causal explanations of the Civil War are legion, and the scope of this book is necessarily limited, it will be enough perhaps to glance at three interestingly different stages in the development of dominant interpretations during the century of dispute intervening since the event.[12] The first is the so-called "conspiracy" theory, which had its heyday during and immediately after the war itself, but which has made something of a comeback in recent years. The second, which in some form or other seems to have held the field from roughly the 1890's to the 1930's, we may call the "conflict" theory, echoing the well-known phrase of W. H.

[11] What follows, with a few minor emendations, was first published as "Some Casual Accounts of the American Civil War," *Daedalus*, XCI, No. 3 (Summer, 1960), 578-92.

[12] For more detailed surveys (to which this account is indebted), see, besides the work of Stampp already noted, Thomas J. Pressly, *Americans Interpret Their Civil War* (Princeton: Princeton University Press, 1954; available in a paperback edition); Lee Benson and Cushing Strout, "Causation and the American Civil War," *History and Theory*, I, No. 2 (1961), 175ff; Howard K. Beale, "What Historians Have Said About the Causes of the Civil War," in *Theory and Practice in Historical Study*, pp. 53-102; Lee Benson and Thomas J. Pressly, "Can Differences in Interpretations of the American Civil War Be Resolved Objectively?" a paper discussed by the American Historical Association, December 29, 1956; and C. W. Ramsdell, "The Changing Interpretation of the Civil War," *Journal of Southern History*, III, No 1 (February, 1937), 3-27.

Seward, "the irrepressible conflict." The third, which appeared in the mid-1930's and is still being actively debated, we may (following the practice of historians themselves) call "revisionist." To sum up the historiography of the Civil War and its causes in three such simple stages, of course, amounts to a great oversimplification. Yet it does reflect actual trends, and it will provide sufficient material for present ana-lytical purposes.

Now even among historians disagreeing sharply about the causes of the Civil War, it must be recognized that there is usually a substantial amount of agreement about what is relevant to a full-scale *understanding* of it. In almost all cases, for example, there will be mentioned a series of incidents such as the Supreme Court decision on the Dred Scott case, John Brown's raid on Harpers Ferry, and the election of Lincoln in 1860 on a minority vote. Attention will also be drawn to various stand-ing conditions such as the antislavery agitation in the North, pressure for re-opening the slave trade in the South, quarreling over enforcement of the fugitive slave law, growing economic tensions between industrial-ists and planters maneuvering for political control of the Democratic party, and so on—not to mention the character, opportunities, and ac-tions of prominent public figures like Seward and Davis, Lincoln and Douglas. All these and a host of other relevant items will normally be woven into a coherent and predominantly narrative account of how the Civil War came to break out, and sometimes without any explicit causal judgments being registered. Yet historians almost always, sooner or later, *single out* certain acts, events, or circumstances from the nar-rative as a whole, as being causes of the coming of the war.[13]

The conspiracy theory   The three theories of Civil War causation already mentioned all involve discriminations of this kind. The conspiracy theory, as the name suggests, selects as cause the actions of certain indi-viduals and groups—the "conspirators." It was a popular theory both during the war itself and during the reconstruction period, not only with avowed propagandists and sensation-seeking journalists, but with serious-minded (if self-taught) historians like Bancroft, Lunt, and Jefferson Davis. When we ask who the conspirators were, however, the value judgment implicit in their selection immediately shows itself in a significant split along sectional lines. To southern historians they were northern abolitionists, out to eradicate the South's "peculiar institution" by the only method possible: the violation of constitutional guarantees after the capture of the federal government; or they were "Black Re-publican" politicians, determined to make use of the slavery issue to

---

[13] Thus Allan Nevins at the end of Volume II of his *Emergence of Lincoln* (New York: Charles Scribner's Sons, 1960) undertakes to single out the "main root of the conflict," which he finds to be "the problem of slavery with its complemen-tary problem of race-adjustment." The "main source of the tragedy," he adds, was the "refusal of either section to face these conjoined problems squarely and pay the heavy cost of a peaceful settlement" (p. 468).

achieve control of the federal government. To northerners the villains were the planters and their political allies, determined to protect slavery by ensuring its spread to the territories, and perhaps ultimately to all the states. As the contemporary historian, George Bancroft, put it, "leading Southern politicians" had engaged "for over a quarter-century in a conspiracy to disrupt the government which they could no longer control." [14] The time seemed to have come when it was necessary to determine by whom the Union was to be run.

Now what sort of dispute is this? There are certainly important nonevaluative points at issue. The case of each side, for example, depends upon the correctness of the attribution of certain motives to the alleged conspirators of the rival section. But even if sectional advocates reach agreement as to the motives and intentions of all the actors, the question remains whether it was the attempt, say, of the northerners to eradicate slavery that caused the war, or the attempt of the southerners to protect it. For the historians of the period, the choice between these possibilities rested on moral grounds: it was based on an appraisal of the reasonableness or degree of justification of the actions of each side; it depended on the answer given to the question: Who was being aggressive and who was simply defending his rights? To southerners, the secession of the South (even the firing on Sumter) was simply a warranted response to a northern threat and was not a cause of the war, even though it was a necessary step in bringing it about and may even have initiated it. To northerners, denying the constitutional right of secession and claiming legal possession of federal property in the states, the cause was southern resistance to rightful occupation—the last act in a series expressing resistance to the idea of the Union. The concept of causation employed by such conspiracy theorists on either side is thus logically tied to the evaluation of those actions which are candidates for causal status. That the actions of either Black Republicans or the slaveholders and their allies were cause of the war is a judgment requiring the prior judgment that these same actions were reprehensible.

There is one form of the conspiracy theory, it should be noted, which escapes the implications of this analysis. It has been asserted by some southern sympathizers, for example, that the actual outbreak of hostilities (if that is what we are trying to explain) was plotted by Lincoln himself, and achieved by sending the relief expedition to Fort Sumter. Lincoln knew, it is argued, that if a federal ship appeared in Charleston harbor, it would be fired on. He sent it so that it *would* be fired on and thus make the South commit itself, not just to secession, but to war. In contesting this form of the conspiracy theory, Kenneth Stampp very properly concentrates entirely on the question of Lincoln's intentions; for the claim that Lincoln caused the war by his policy at Sumter could not be denied if it could be established that he acted while knowing and intending this result. Stampp relieves Lincoln's in-

[14] Pressly, *Americans Interpret Their Civil War*, p. 8.

tervention of causal status on the ground that the President's calculation was rather that his own position, previously weak, would be secured whether the Confederate batteries opened fire or not.[15] If they did fire, he would have a united North behind him; and if they did not, the Confederacy would be weakened by failing to stand on its alleged sovereign rights.

If partisans of South or North disagree about Lincoln's motives and intentions, this may still be due to their evaluative commitments, in the sense that they are not in fact (although they should be) equally swayed by the same evidence. Nevertheless, the question of Lincoln's motivation can still be decided in principle, without the logical involvement of such an evaluation. Few of the conspiracy theorists, however, have gone so far as to attribute the Civil War to the deliberate plan or plot of certain agents. The supposed conspiracies were usually aimed at something short of war, and their role as causes, therefore, has to be established more subtly. This is done in the value-charged way already indicated.

The conflict theory   Following the first outburst of writing on the Civil War, mainly by apologists and partisans, there was a gradual shift of interpretation from conspiracy to what might be called "conflict" theories. Historians in both sections, especially in the North, tended to realize that there were two sides to the quarrel, and that an understanding of what happened required an adequate treatment of both. They therefore came to look with more sympathy on the motives and aims of their erstwhile opponents and to be more circumspect in allotting blame. As a result, the actions of the other side, or of its significant minorities, gradually lost causal status. The men of both sides came to be thought of, in a sense, as being trapped in a situation not entirely of their own making, one allowing them little room for maneuver. As Howard K. Beale puts it, they came to see the war "not as a conspiracy of one group but as a struggle between two groups with irreconcilable interests." [16] The cause was then sought in the situation itself—the conditions presenting such a difficult problem—rather than in the responses of the various actors to it.

Historians still differed, it should be noted, on the proper characterization of the problem situation; and their accounts, at any rate at first, tended once again to divide along sectional lines. Thus J. F. Rhodes, a northern historian of the Nineties, declares: "Of the American Civil War it may safely be asserted that there was a single cause, slavery. . . . The whole dispute really hinged on the belief of the South

---

[15] *And the War Came* (Baton Rouge: Louisiana State University Press, 1950), pp. 285-86.

[16] Beale, "What Historians Have Said About the Causes of the Civil War," *op. cit.*, p. 61.

that slavery was right and the belief of the majority of Northerners that it was wrong." [17] Rhodes does not, however, like most of his northern predecessors, use his personal agreement with the northern view to justify his attribution of causal status to the actions of the other side. The cause of the war was not the wrongheaded determination of the South to keep or extend the institution; the cause was not what anyone *did* about slavery; it was *the fact that it was there at all.* Slavery, according to Rhodes, was "the calamity of Southern men, not their crime." [18] The South was certainly mistaken; but Rhodes is far too conscious of wrongdoing on both sides to hinge a causal judgment on such a one-sided attribution of blame.

In the South a whole generation of historians tended to agree with Jefferson Davis that the struggle was not essentially one between two moral codes but one between two schools of constitutional interpretation.[19] The North, for whatever reason, had gradually lost sight of the concept of federal union animating the Constitution devised by the Fathers—a concept ensuring the highest degree of autonomy in the states, which in theory retained their sovereignty. Differences of economic and political interest in North and South were natural and unexceptional; and it was to make it possible for the two sections to live together in spite of these differences that the powers of the federal government were limited. Slavery was only one of a number of issues which brought this difference in the basic interpretation of the Union into question. For two groups with such irreconcilable constitutional views to continue in a single state was unthinkable; separation, in view of the same issue, was likewise impossible without war. Once again, although the historian in fact thinks one side in the dispute to be in the wrong, he deliberately excludes that moral judgment from his explanatory account. The consequent attempt to see the struggle in a detached way, and from both sides, again results in transferring causal status from the actions to the situation itself.

Now it may perhaps be thought that at this point, which is also the point at which we begin to hear about the "scientific" historiography of the Civil War,[20] historians succeed in separating their causal judgments from their value judgments altogether. Yet the causal judgment, it might surely be argued, is still in part evaluative; for it still selects one relevant factor (the problem situation) and rejects another (what the agents did in response to it); and this selection is presumably based on some criterion or principle. The conflict theorist selects the predicament itself as cause because he judges that no course of action that could reasonably have been expected from the men of either side would have

[17] *Lectures on the Civil War*, reprinted in Stampp, *Causes*, pp. 107, 108.
[18] Pressly, *Americans Interpret Their Civil War*, p. 143.
[19] *Ibid.*, p. 64.
[20] *Ibid.*, p. 152.

succeeded in avoiding war. And the word "reasonable" which enters here is crucial to an understanding of what is being claimed. For the conflict theorist need not deny, for example, that the war could have been avoided by the North's abandoning the western territories to slavery, or by the South's capitulation to the demands of the Union government before the firing on Fort Sumter. He simply does not demand such heroic responses from ordinary human beings; he is less exacting in his standards than the conspiracy theorist. In locating the cause of the war in the fact that the problems facing the actors were "beyond them," he is guided nevertheless by moral considerations as surely as is the partisan of the conspiracy interpretation.

The only way to avoid such a conclusion would be to interpret the conflict theory as representing the problem situation as a *sufficient condition* of the Civil War—and the war itself, consequently, as inevitable. It must be admitted that there has been a tendency in that direction among conflict theorists. With the rise of the trained historian in the late 1890's and the great increase in the scope of historical interests, the account of the nature of the struggle has tended to broaden. Newer southern historians like Wilson, for example, having disposed of the moral question by observing that both sides in the constitutional struggle were "right" from their own points of view, seek causes in the social and economic conditions which explain how each came to the point of view in question.[21] Northern historians like F. J. Turner and Edward Channing also discover causes in the historical processes which had made the two sections so different.[22] By the end of World War I, the Beards were representing the war as a "triumph of industry over agriculture," and its cause as an economic conflict so basic that "the transfer of the issues from the forum to the field . . . was bound to come." [23] In 1934 A. C. Cole further generalized the struggle by picturing "two different civilizations contesting, one for supremacy and the other for independence." [24] Insofar as such accounts really mean that the war could not have been avoided by any means, given the nature of the conflict, then the element of value judgment in the causal conclusion has disappeared. Yet in spite of what may seem to be the contrary implications of their language, few conflict theorists are really willing to be pushed to such a conclusion. As one of their most recent champions, Pieter Geyl, has put it, the problem of slavery for the men of the time was "overwhelming"; but this does not imply "that the war was inevitable, not even . . . in the ten years preceding the outbreak." [25]

[21] *Ibid.*, p. 171.

[22] *Ibid.*, pp. 177, 180.

[23] Charles and Mary Beard, *The Rise of American Civilization* (New York: The Macmillan Company, 1927), II, 10, 54.

[24] *Irrepressible Conflict, 1850–1865* (New York: The Macmillan Company, 1934), p. xiii.

[25] "The American Civil War and the Problem of Inevitability," reprinted in Stampp, *Causes*, p. 122.

To argue that the selection of causes is partly evaluative, even in the case of historians offering apparently detached "conflict" interpretations, may perhaps appear to read more into their accounts than they intended. If so, it may be of interest to point out that distinguished members of the historical profession have not hesitated to do the same. For the third sort of interpretation to be noted is a reaction against the second on precisely the sort of ground which has been sketched. The "revisionism" of the 1930's, exemplified in particular by the work of Avery Craven and J. G. Randall, loudly protests what it considers to be the moral flabbiness of the conflict theory. Its rival causal claims are advanced on the ground that historians must reassert human responsibility for what occurred, and must make clear the extent to which the Civil War was a "needless" one.

The willingness of the revisionists to apportion blame, however, does not signalize a return to the sectional type of partisanship. For moral judgment now cuts *across* sectional divisions and singles out guilty parties and groups on both sides of the quarrel (although there is admittedly a certain tendency—perhaps a compensatory one—to deal more harshly with the North). To the revisionists, the heroes are the exponents of compromise on both sides of the line—men like Douglas and Buchanan. What overwhelmed them and brought on the tragedy was (in Randall's words) "emotional unreason and overbold leadership." "If one word or phrase were selected to account for the war," Randall writes, "that word would not be slavery, or economic grievance, or state rights, or diverse civilizations. It would have to be such a word as fanaticism (on both sides), misunderstanding, misrepresentation, or perhaps politics." [26] Craven assesses the situation in similar terms. The war, he says, was the work of "a generation of well-meaning Americans, who . . . permitted their short-sighted politicians, their over-zealous editors and their pious reformers to emotionalize real and potential differences, and to conjure up distorted impressions of those who dwelt in other parts of the nation." [27]

As T. N. Bonner explains it, what the revisionists are reacting against is "a view which exposes human helplessness in a web of our own making." [28] They are very much aware of the fact that the concentration upon conflict as a cause implies that the war, although perhaps not inevitable, was still not something men could reasonably have been expected to avoid. The revisionists' abhorrence of war (to Randall it is "organized murder" [29]) was so great that they, by contrast, were willing to blame the actors for behaving in perfectly familiar and understandable ways—for failing, in other words, to rise to the occasion. The war, Craven insists, was not an "irrepressible conflict"; we *could*

---

[26] "A Blundering Generation," reprinted in Stampp, *Causes*, pp. 85-86.
[27] Quoted in T. N. Bonner, "Civil War Historians and the 'Needless War' Doctrine," *Journal of the History of Ideas*, XVII, No. 2 (April, 1956), 199.
[28] "Civil War Historians and the 'Needless War' Doctrine," *op. cit.*, p. 216.
[29] Quoted in Pressly, *Americans Interpret Their Civil War*, p. 274.

have expected something better from the protagonists; for *"it is the statesman's business* to compromise issues until a people have grown to higher levels where problems solve themselves." [30] The war, he insists, was "needless" and "avoidable." Because it *could* have been avoided, it *should* have been. Because it nevertheless occurred, we must look for its causes in the actions of those who failed to prevent it.

Critics of the revisionists, like A. M. Schlesinger, Jr. and Pieter Geyl, have scoffed at the naïveté which expects such a standard of rationality in human affairs. Surely by now, Geyl writes, we have given up the belief that man is "a sensible being" [31]—thereby suggesting (in spite of his own disclaimer) that, given such a conflict situation, war was inevitable after all. Revisionists have also, and more characteristically, been attacked for seeming to imply that only in an emotional frenzy could the majority of men have gone to war over the slavery issue. This, say their critics, reveals a failure of understanding. "By denying themselves insight into the moral dimensions of slavery," Schlesinger charges, "the revisionists denied themselves a historical understanding of the intensities that caused the crisis." "To reject the moral actuality of the Civil War," he continues, "is to foreclose the possibility of an adequate account of its causes." [32]

One might, of course, interpret the latter criticism simply as charging that the revisionists failed correctly to interpret the motives, the rational calculations, of both sides—failed to see, for example, that the historical agents concerned might really have been acting for explicable moral reasons, rather than out of political calculation or an induced paroxysm of emotion. This might be thought to raise only nonevaluative issues concerning the interpretation of motives. In enlarging on the reasons for this alleged failure of understanding, however, the critics generally shift their ground. By such phrases as "the moral actuality of the Civil War," they mean to imply that North and South could not reasonably have been asked to compose their differences peacefully; they evince their conviction that there are certain things *worth fighting for.* "Because the revisionists felt no moral urgency themselves [regarding slavery]," writes Schlesinger, "they deplored as fanatics those who did feel it, or brushed aside their feelings as the artificial product of emotion and propaganda." [33] The situation in which the men of the 1860's found themselves, he continues, involved "moral differences too profound to be solved by compromise." A return to a version of the conflict theory is thus urged: the actions of both sides, because they were genuinely responses to what appeared as moral imperatives, are regarded as "forced" by something else—the unhappy situation itself.

[30] Quoted in Bonner, "Civil War Historians and the 'Needless War' Doctrine," *op. cit.*, p. 209. My italics.
[31] "The American Civil War and the Problem of Inevitability," *op. cit.*, p. 121.
[32] "The Causes of the Civil War: A Note on Historical Sentimentalism," reprinted in Stampp, *Causes*, pp. 116, 117.
[33] *Ibid.*, p. 116.

It is the latter, therefore, which is the cause. Whether revisionists or their critics are to be accepted as giving the better account of the causes of the Civil War is not the point at issue here. Our problem is simply to see what, in differing about causation, they are really quarrelling about. And that is surely the stand to be taken on a moral issue: whether war with one's fellow countrymen is a greater moral evil than acquiescence in political and economic domination, or in the continuance of an institution like chattel slavery.

If the foregoing examples of causal judgment in history are at all representative—and surely they are—it should now be clear why historians will never know "objectively" what caused the Civil War—why, in Stampp's words, "after a century of enormous effort the debate is still inconclusive." The reason lies at least partly in the concept of causation historians employ. They use the term "cause" in such a way that their value judgments are relevant to their causal conclusions—not just in the sense that they do in fact influence those conclusions, but in the sense that the conclusions are logically dependent on them. As long as "cause" is not to mean "sufficient condition," there must be some reason for singling out one relevant condition of what happened from the others. In the cases we have examined, at least, the historian's reason appears to derive from moral considerations. It is from the standpoint of moral appraisal (rather than that of manipulability, for example) that his causal judgment is made.

Abnormality and   There are a number of ways such a conclusion might be chal-
voluntariness   lenged. To be constructive, a challenge should try to offer an
alternative analysis of the causal judgments historians make, which accounts for their differences by reference to nonmoral criteria of selection. A number of such alternatives have in fact been offered besides Collingwood's seemingly inappropriate criterion of practical, manipulative interest. Of these we may consider briefly, in concluding this chapter, an impressively worked out account offered by H. L. A. Hart and A. M. Honoré.[34] This is presented primarily as throwing light on causal judgments in the law. But it is specifically said to be applicable also to judgments typically made by historians.

According to Hart and Honoré, the criteria for selecting causal conditions, in everyday life and as well as in history and the law, can be reduced to two. The first is that causes are abnormalities, although the concept of the "normal" varies subtly from context to context. The second is that voluntary human actions, being *ex hypothesi* themselves uncaused, have a special claim to causal status. Both of these notions

---

[34] H. L. A. Hart and A. M. Honoré, *Causation in the Law* (New York: Oxford University Press, 1959). For other accounts of the selection of causal conditions, see Gardiner, *The Nature of Historical Explanation*, pp. 99ff; R. M. MacIver, *Social Causation* (Boston: Ginn & Company, 1942), pp. 160ff; and Ernest Nagel, "Some Issues in the Logic of Historical Analysis," in *The Philosophy of History in Our Time*, ed. Meyerhoff, pp. 282ff.

have an obvious connection with what might be thought of as the primitive experience which gives the concept of causation a meaning for us: the experience of interrupting the course of nature, and thus, to an extent, imposing our wills upon it. Looked at from two different sides, our own causal activity is both an intervention and an abnormality—something we deliberately *do*, and hence something not otherwise to have been expected.

In explaining the way the concept of "abnormality" guides causal selection, Hart and Honoré point out that, in the investigation of human affairs, what we usually want to explain is itself some deviation from the ordinary or expected course of events. And it is entirely natural that we should try to explain an abnormality by an abnormality. In human contexts, however, what counts as "the ordinary course of events" may at the same time be something highly contrived. It will often obtain because of certain procedures, long since become customary, which have altered an original course of nature to serve human purposes. When such a customary norm breaks down, it is often some deviation from the protective customary procedures, now regarded as a relevant antecedent abnormality, which is selected as the cause of the breakdown. And a cause will thus often be an omission which coincides with what is reprehensible by established standards of conduct. But this, the authors contend, "does not justify the conclusion which some have drawn that it is so selected merely because it is reprehensible." [35] If the flowers in the garden wither, we may select the gardener's failure to water them as cause. But we can do this, it seems, only because it is customary (i.e., normal) for gardeners to water flowers, and the failure is thus a relevant abnormality.

But, we may ask, is it really just because we expected the gardener to perform his duties, in the predictive sense of "expect," that we regard his failure as the cause? If expectation comes into it, is it not rather in the prescriptive sense of the word? We cite the omission as cause, surely, because flower-watering was to be expected of a gardener; it is what he *ought to have done*. In a similar way, the revisionist historian Avery Craven supports his causal conclusion with the judgment that it is the statesman's *business* to seek compromise. One might surely doubt, too, that the northern conspiracy theorist's causal conclusion entails a belief on his part that the institution of slavery was abnormal in the sense of being not customary. Is it not, rather, that he regards it as abnormal in a value-charged sense? It is true that historians themselves sometimes make use of the concept of "abnormality" in a way which might be thought to vindicate the contention of Hart and Honoré. Thus Stampp writes: " 'revisionist' historians apparently believe that pre-Civil War political leaders were unusually incompetent, that their acts and decisions were grotesque and abnormal. Their exaggeration of sectional differences, their invention of allegedly fictitious issues (such as slavery

[35] *Causation in the Law*, p. 35.

expansion) created a crisis that was highly artificial and eventually pre-cipitated a 'needless' war." [36] But, as the coupling with "grotesque" and "incompetent" suggests, the term "abnormal" is scarcely used here in a purely descriptive sense. This is even clearer in Randall's own revisionist use of it. "Omit the element of abnormality, of *bogus* leadership, or *inordinate* ambition for conquest," he says, "and diagnosis fails." [37]

The second principle of selection proposed by Hart and Honoré may appear to be more acceptable. The notion of voluntary action as cause well accords with both our ordinary notion of a cause as "active," and our tendency to regard causes as "interventions." [38] Clearly, if a man hands over his purse at gunpoint, it is to the actions of the gunman that we look for the cause of his loss, not to his own reluctant response. The principle that, of a number of relevant human actions, the most voluntary one is to be selected as the cause may also appear to throw considerable light on some of the historical judgments we have already examined. Certainly, it seems to be the view of northern and southern historians holding the conspiracy theory that the actions of the other side's extremists were causes, while the responses of the men of their own section were not, because the latter were "forced" by the former, and in that respect were not fully voluntary. In each case, the noncausal responses are represented as responses to threats. As T. J. Pressly puts the southern position: "When Lincoln's intention to reinforce the fort became known, no alternative remained for the Confederates but to capture the fort." [39] The principle might also be brought to bear on what is claimed by conflict theorists, for in this case, it might be claimed, the reason the actions of neither North nor South are causes is that neither can properly be regarded as voluntary. Given the situation they were faced with, neither side was "free" to solve the problem without war. "The unhappy fact," writes Schlesinger, "is that man occasionally works himself into a log-jam; and that the log-jam must be burst by violence." [40]

For present purposes, there is only one thing which needs to be pointed out to anyone accepting this analysis, and that is that the concept of a voluntary action, as Hart and Honoré (correctly) employ it, is itself a quasi-moral concept. As they put it, it is the concept of an action which is not "defective" in any of a miscellaneous number of ways.[41] And to determine whether an action is thus defective, it is necessary to decide whether the agent faced such problems as that of self-preservation (which raises the question of the reasonableness of regarding something as a threat to a vital interest), or of safeguarding the rights of himself or others (which requires the use of moral criteria

[36] Stampp, *Causes*, p. 82.
[37] "A Blundering Generation," *op. cit.*, p. 84. My italics.
[38] *Causation in the Law*, pp. 38ff.
[39] Pressly, *Americans Intepret Their Civil War*, p. 63.
[40] "Causes of the Civil War," *op. cit.*, p. 117.
[41] *Causation in the Law*, pp. 38-39.

outside narrowly legal contexts), or of honoring pressing obligations (which might, once again, be moral as well as legal). It seems to be admitted that at the point where we must decide whether what was done was a reasonable step to have taken in the circumstances—for example, whether it was the "lesser of two evils"—the concept of a fully voluntary action "incorporates" (although indirectly) judgments of value.[42] It would surely follow that causal judgments using this criterion of selection would likewise incorporate judgments of value. And to say that they incorporate them, is not just to say that the two judgments happen to coincide.

[42] *Ibid.*, p. 147.

PHILOSOPHIES OF HISTORY

5

The argument
so far Up to this point we have been concerned to look at some of the issues which commonly arise in critical philosophy of history, and in particular at arguments relevant to the question whether history should be classified among the sciences. What has been said certainly cannot claim to have settled this matter. Any worthwhile attempt to do so would have had to begin with a much more rigorous and detailed account of what it is to be a science than could have been attempted here. And such an account, if it really tried to do justice to the wide range of ostensibly different sorts of inquiries usually called scientific, would in any case probably not have given us any simple or single answer to our question. What *may* be claimed is that the arguments considered do draw attention to features of historical inquiry which are usually either ignored or underemphasized by those philosophers who characteristically insist that history is, or ought to be, scientific. Those features (to recapitulate) are a mode of explanation which does not obviously proceed by subsumption under general laws; an approach to the construction of a history which includes a concern for "assessment" as well as mere "truth-telling"; and a concept of causal connection which involves moral as well as inductive considerations. It is features of this sort which often lead theorists of historical inquiry to claim that history belongs to the humanities rather than to the sciences. What critical philosophy of history must make clear is the extent, if any, to which such features can be represented as part of the *structure* of the inquiry—derivable, that is, from its "idea"—rather than just *facts*, interesting or otherwise, about the way most historians happen to operate.

As was indicated in Chapter 1, however, such issues have not, for most of its career, formed the main stuff of what has been called philosophy of history. They have in fact emerged from time to time—for example, in the writings of a Vico or a Hegel—but only as ancillary to the main item of interest: a philosophical account of history, not as a branch of inquiry, but as a process: the actual course of events. Such speculative accounts have generally claimed that there is in historical events a "significance" or "meaning" which goes beyond the understanding ordinarily sought by historians. In turning to consider this side of the subject in the remainder of the book, the problem of what to attempt by way of introduction is perhaps even more acute than it was in the earlier part; for to do justice to any one of the great speculative systems of history is clearly beyond the present compass, while to discuss the problems of such system-building without reference to examples of it would seem to put the cart before the horse. By way of compromise, in the remaining chapters outlines will be presented of some of the main doctrines of three well-known authors of speculative systems: the German idealist philosopher, G. W. F. Hegel; the English historian (or "metahistorian" [1]), Arnold Toynbee; and the American theologian, Reinhold Niebuhr. Each outline will be given to a large extent in the author's own terms, and will be followed by a few critical comments. The present chapter will preface this with a short account of the development of philosophy of history in the speculative sense, and a preliminary indication of its nature, kinds, and aspects.

Some interest in history on the part of philosophers can, of course, be traced back to the very beginnings of their subject. It is present, for example, in Platonic and Aristotelian theories about the way forms of government characteristically succeed each other in the state. History was scarcely a dominant theme, however, in any philosophy before that of Augustine, and there is little subsequently of very great interest before the early eighteenth century speculations of the Italian philosopher Vico. The neglect of Vico's work by his contemporaries, who were still concerned mainly with absorbing the lessons of post-Renaissance natural science, justifies the usual practice of regarding the rise of philosophy of history as a serious study as the work of the late eighteenth and early nineteenth centuries: the work chiefly of the German idealists, Kant, Herder, Fichte, and Hegel. Significantly, this was also a period in which independent interest in historical studies proper was growing rapidly— a development which culminated in the emergence of history in the nineteenth century as a *discipline*, self-consciously pursued, with its own methods, concepts, and professional guardians.

Yet the first flowering of speculative philosophy of history was also,

[1] For the use of this label by historians, see F. H. Underhill, "Arnold Toynbee: Metahistorian," *Canadian Historical Review*, XXXII, No. 3 (September, 1951), 201-19; and Christopher Dawson, "The Problem of Metahistory," *History Today*, I, No. 6 (June, 1951), 9-11.

in a sense, its last. Never after Hegel were its claims so bold, or so brilliantly presented. The nineteenth century saw a number of more pedestrian attempts to get the measure of history as a whole—those of Comte and Spencer, for example; and it continued to feel the impact of Hegel through Marx. But the very development of first-order historical studies, to which the rise of speculation originally owed so much, in the end raised serious problems for it. For it became more and more difficult to represent speculative constructions as soundly based in the light of increasingly critical standards for the acceptance of historical fact. Twentieth century system builders like Toynbee and Spengler have made notable attempts to meet this kind of criticism; and there is little doubt that Toynbee, in particular, has at his disposal a range of historical data which has never been approached in the history of speculation. Unfortunately, this has scarcely been matched with corresponding philosophical insight. Our own century has also seen a lively recrudescence of more straightforwardly religious attempts to declare the "meaning" of history: an approach which had gone out of style with the Enlightenment. The work of Niebuhr exemplifies this latter development.

Kinds of systems   These historical remarks draw attention to a way in which speculative philosophies of history are sometimes classified: by reference to the "source of authority" or final basis of argument they recognize. The systems of Hegel, Toynbee, and Niebuhr differ markedly in this regard; they are (or at least claim to be), respectively, metaphysically, empirically, and religiously based. Thus the meaning Hegel finds in the course of history can only fully be expounded by means of metaphysical notions like "World Spirit," which are derived from his general philosophical position. And the acceptability of his account depends, in the end, upon the acceptability of that position as a whole. Toynbee's view of history, by contrast, is represented as a conclusion forced upon him by an empirical survey. And at least part of it, the assertion of certain historical laws, claims a status analogous to that of an empirically validated scientific hypothesis. Niebuhr is so much at odds with both of these approaches that at times he denies that he offers, in any comparable sense, a "philosophy" of history at all. He claims only to show how Christian faith, which transcends rational argument, can give a meaning to otherwise meaningless occurrences. He nevertheless appears to be thoroughly involved in the issues raised by the other two approaches. For he denies that metaphysical reflection or empirical investigation can make sense of history at all.

A more usual way of classifying philosophies of history is by the type of pattern they claim to find in past events. At the most general level of analysis, there are, of course, only three possibilities open. Either history will be found to have a *linear* pattern—it will be "going somewhere"; or it will be *cyclical*, repeating itself endlessly in succeeding peoples and periods; or it will appear *chaotic*, exhibiting (as H. A. L. Fisher puts it) only "the play of the contingent and the unforeseen." [2] A linear account may, of course, be progressive *or* regressive. Most linear theories, however—those of Condorcet and Kant are examples—have in fact asserted human progress.

Various combinations of the basic possibilities may also be encountered. A cyclical development may be linked with a linear one to form the kind of spiraling advance asserted by Vico in his *New Science*. A theory which is chaotic at one level may admit fragmentary developments of either cyclical or linear type at another. Thus, according to Spengler, civilizations spring up willy-nilly; but each, once started, follows a "normal" career. Actually, few philosophies of history can be classified without qualification as linear, cyclical, or chaos theories; and this is true of the three whose chief doctrines we are to examine. Hegel, for example, although he emphasizes the linear development of human freedom in history, finds a recurring three-stage pattern in the stories of the various peoples who contribute thereto. And Toynbee, who, at any rate at first, sees history in terms of the rise and fall of civilizations, in the end comes to represent this as contributing cumulatively to the spiritual insight of the human race. Even Niebuhr, who finds no significant over-all pattern, and who is selected here in part because he comes so close to being a "chaos" theorist, admits that one can draw lines of progress through the past: the line of technological advance, for example. But he cannot see that any of these pick out developments of much importance from the standpoint of Christian faith.

Maurice Mandelbaum employs a principle of classification which brings out further interesting features of speculative systems.[3] Holding that all philosophy of history seeks to discover meaning by finding the "most basic factor operative within history," he distinguishes between "two fundamentally different forms" which such a factor may take. The more common form is a "law of history" which explains historical change. Such laws are either "linear" or "morphological" (Mandelbaum's term for "cyclical"). Both state an "invariant tendency of history"; they are explanatory because they render the actual course of history inevitable, whether this course is directional or recursive. The second fundamental form is that of an "explanatory concept which is held to be applicable to each and every crucial event in the historical process," and to offer a basis for regarding it as meaningful *whatever the course of events may be*. According to Mandelbaum, a simple providential theory which regards whatever happens as "the will of God" would

---

[2] *A History of Europe* (Toronto: Longmans, Green & Company, 1936), p. v.
[3] "Some Neglected Philosophic Problems Regarding History," *Journal of Philosophy*, XLIX, No. 10 (May 8, 1952), 317-28. See also his "A Critique of Philosophies of History," *Journal of Philosophy*, XLV, No. 14 (July 1, 1948), 365-78; and "Concerning Recent Trends in the Theory of Historiography," *Journal of the History of Ideas*, XVI, No. 4 (October, 1955), 506-17.

be an example of this: history is regarded as meaningful because of the "omnipresence" of the divine in it.

Mandelbaum's distinction between linear and morphological theories obviously has affinities with the one already noted between two sorts of pattern-drawing. The chief difference lies in his equation of historical patterns and historical laws. As Mandelbaum goes on to show, the concept of law envisaged here is a difficult one. Its employment would make speculative laws of history quite unlike the general assertions usually found in the natural or social sciences. Rather than stating "invariant relations within history," which could be expressed hypothetically in the form "If C then E," they would state categorically the invariant *trend* of the historical series as a whole. In a discussion of the same point, K. R. Popper has roundly accused speculative philosophy of history of systematically confusing the notions of laws and trends.[4] Mandelbaum, on the other hand, points out that even scientists sometimes assert "necessary trends" as laws—the law of entropy in physics being an example. What he questions is the possibility of claiming knowledge of such laws when we are not "dealing with self-transformations within a single closed system"—as in history, he thinks it obvious, we are not.

What Mandelbaum and Popper have to say does draw attention to a genuine logical problem of some speculative philosophies. Since it is doubtful, however, that any of our sample theorists assert the trend they find in history as a "law"—Toynbee's laws, for example, appear to be formulable in the hypothetical way (insofar as they are formulable at all)—perhaps this matter need not be pursued further here. Mandelbaum's second distinction, however, between theories which explain by pattern (necessary or otherwise) and those which explain by concept, is of special interest for our discussion. For, as he observes himself, Niebuhr's view of history, with its notion that "in every historically significant event there is a tension between opposing pulls in human nature" (this being elucidated in theological terms), may be interpreted as belonging to the second type. For such a theorist, the "meaning" attributed to history is not, strictly speaking, found in the *course* of events at all.

Three questions　As the foregoing remarks will have indicated, speculative systems fall into different kinds or classes on a number of important principles. Their answers to the question "Has history any meaning?" in fact vary so widely that it has sometimes been doubted that they all interpret the *question* in the same way. In any critical examination of speculation, however, it is equally important to recognize that, even within a single system, this vague governing question breaks down into more determinate, component ones. And a philosopher's answer to one

[4] *The Poverty of Historicism* (Boston: Beacon Press, Inc., 1957), pp. 41ff, 105ff.

of these may often be deemed more satisfactory than the answer he gives to others.

Clearly, the first component question which speculative philosophers ask is what the *pattern* of the past has been. Linear, cyclical, and chaos theories are, in the first instance at least, answers to this. It might be noted that, as it stands, this question is not the sort we should ordinarily regard as especially "philosophical." For historians, too, look for patterns in the events they study. It is true they generally select some subject, theme, or period less extensive than the whole of the human past, whereas speculative philosophers of history do not limit themselves in this way. Yet, as our earlier discussion of selection should have shown, to ask whether history as a whole has a theme, although it goes beyond the usual interests of historians, does not, in principle at any rate, go beyond the canons of ordinary historical inquiry.

This point is especially worth mention at a time when many historians are reacting against what they have come to regard as the rather limited approach to history of their immediate predecessors: their applying to their work, for example, a narrowly European standard of importance. Apropos of this, Geoffrey Barraclough has recently argued that, even though historians can seldom, in practice, attempt to deal with more than some chosen fragment of universal history, they should try nevertheless to write their accounts "from a universal point of view." [5] If historical writing becomes, in this way, less provincial, we may well regard this as an improvement. It should be clear, however, that by thus enlarging their viewpoint, historians will not necessarily become philosophers of history. For the same reason, universal history is not philosophy simply because it is (and has generally had to be) written by philosophers. At *any* level, whether the past displays a certain pattern is a historical question. This is as true for cyclical patterns as for linear ones, insofar as the patterns are simply asserted to obtain. And it is true no matter how bizarre the patterns proposed by speculative philosophers may sometimes appear to professional historians.

But speculative philosophers of history do not, of course, confine themselves to asserting patterns as historical facts. They do not even confine themselves to giving historical explanations of them. In addition, they usually claim to discover *in general* how historical change takes place; they try to solve the problem of the *mechanism* of history. To assert that historical events instantiate a law or a body of laws is to give one sort of answer to this second component question. Insofar as the laws assume the form of empirically verifiable hypotheses, this aspect of the speculative theorist's inquiry will, of course, be continuous in "idea" with science—just as, at the level of pattern-drawing, the inquiry is continuous with ordinary history. And it may well have to be conceded, as its critics sometimes maintain, that in this aspect speculative philosophy of history can be no more than a rough, exploratory

[5] "Universal History," in *Approaches to History*, ed. Finberg, pp. 83-109.

sort of inquiry: it is "science," but only in embryo. As such it is something that ought to be superseded by the social sciences proper as the latter come to maturity.

Not all speculative responses to the mechanism question, however, are obviously reducible to the assertion of empirical laws. Some try rather to state in very general terms what might be called the basic causal factors of the historical process. Marx's distinction between substructural and superstructural features of a society, and his claim that the former have explanatory primacy, is a case in point. Such accounts might well be susceptible to further analysis along the lines of our discussion of causation in Chapter 4. Whether they are or not, what they offer seems to be less a law, yielding specific explanations, than a kind of schematic *model* showing how all acceptable explanations in the field must go. In some such cases, it should be noted, the philosopher's question yields answers for which "mechanism" may be too determinate, not to say deterministic, a notion. The Hegelian idea that historical advance is "dialectical," that it takes place through a series of tensions and resolutions which exhibit some rational or logical order, is such a one. Toynbee's formula of "challenge-and-response" and Niebuhr's all-pervasive "original sin" are others—as is Spengler's concept of a quasi-biological "destiny" built into social organisms. As W. H. Walsh observes, such theories have two connected features (besides an inordinate tendency to vagueness) which may lead people to call them "philosophical": they are usually held with much greater conviction than any available empirical evidence would seem to warrant; and they are usually bound up with some general conception of the nature of man and the world.[6]

Whether laws or explanatory models are asserted, it is clear that in passing from the question of "pattern" to that of "mechanism" the speculative philosopher goes beyond historical inquiry altogether. His transcendence of ordinary history becomes even more obvious, however, when, as he usually does, he goes on to ask still another question: what *purpose* or *value* or *justification* can be found for a process having the pattern and mechanism history is alleged to have. At this point speculation becomes inseparable from metaphysics, ethics, and religion. It is significant in this connection that, although only Niebuhr, of our three chosen examples, declares himself frankly to be looking to religion for a clue to the "meaning" of history, the other two accounts are also in their own ways thoroughly religious. For Hegel, the aim of speculative philosophy of history is "theodicy—justification of the ways of God," so that we may be "reconciled with the fact of the existence of evil." For Toynbee, the problem is how any spiritually significant purpose can be served by the "vain repetitions" of the cyclic life of civilizations.

In view of this third sort of concern, the distinction adopted in this book between metaphysical, religious, and empirical theories may

[6] *Philosophy of History: An Introduction*, pp. 103-4.

be somewhat misleading. For it is difficult to see what would count as a purely *empirical* answer to the question of the purpose of history: an answer that was not at the same time metaphysical or religious. By "empirical philosophy of history," perhaps all that can legitimately be meant is a system which places special emphasis upon showing the known details of history to be compatible with the purpose being attributed; or one in which the philosopher approaches historical data without a pre-formulated hypothesis, and tries to let the data themselves at least suggest answers to his questions. On such criteria, Toynbee's account could properly be called empirical by contrast with the others. Whatever the degree of its empirical emphasis, however, no speculative philosophy of history which raises the third component question stands or falls by reference to historical facts alone. *All* depend upon the acceptability of the total "world view" of their authors, whether this is grounded in the rationalistic arguments of a Hegel, the mystical musings of a Toynbee, or the theological dogmas of a Niebuhr.

The chapters which follow will make little attempt to pursue criticism or appraisal into this wider context. It will be deemed sufficient for the purpose of this introduction to try to show how each philosopher answers the questions of pattern, mechanism, and purpose, how these answers fit together, whether they are in themselves intelligible and self-consistent, and what their relationship is to the conclusions of ordinary history. In doing this, we shall be undertaking an inquiry analogous to that of the first part of this book: we shall be trying to clarify the "idea" of speculative philosophy of history. But we shall be doing this by a more indirect method: the exposition of, and comment upon, examples of it.

A METAPHYSICAL APPROACH

6

G. W. F. Hegel   "The expression, 'philosophy of history,' " observes Patrick Gardiner, "has come to have various associations. By some it may be
regarded as signifying a submarine monster, dredged from the deep
waters of nineteenth century metaphysics, its jaws occasionally opening
to emit prophecies in a dead (or at any rate foreign) tongue—the
language of Hegelian dialectic." [1] As this quotation suggests, in choosing
to include the Hegelian system in an introductory discussion, we are
undoubtedly taking risks. It is not for nothing that Hegel has long
served in some quarters as the very symbol of the shortcomings of
speculative philosophy generally. His thought is tortuous; his language is
both technical and obscure. He has the temerity to put everything in
its place—even logic, with which he is often accused of playing fast and
loose. Yet the choice of his system, as illustrating a distinctively metaphysical approach, is so natural as to be almost unavoidable. Even those
who like neither his manner nor his conclusions often admit that Hegel
was a powerful thinker, with whose doctrines it is necessary to come to
grips.[2] Few philosophers, furthermore—and none of the first rank—have
devoted so much of their attention to history. As R. G. Collingwood
puts it, in Hegel's work "history for the first time steps out full-grown
on the stage of philosophical thought." [3] Certainly all parts of his
philosophy are permeated with a historical interest. In return, his own
influence on historical studies, especially on the history of ideas, has
been enormous.

Hegel's status as a great metaphysician, however, raises special
difficulties for any attempt to put simply and shortly his chief conten-

[1] *The Nature of Historical Explanation*, p. ix.
[2] For a good introduction in this vein, see C. J. Friedrich's Preface to *The Philosophy of Hegel* (New York: Modern Library, Inc., 1958).
[3] *The Idea of History*, p. 113.

tions about history. For these are thoroughly integrated within a philosophy of extraordinary comprehensiveness, connectedness, and complication. His theory of history is embedded in his political philosophy—itself an integral part of a whole philosophy of mind or spirit. And few Hegelians would allow that what he says about history can be appreciated fully in isolation from the rest. Yet there exists a work of Hegel's, posthumously published, which is concerned exclusively with outlining his view of human history. And in his Introduction to these *Lectures on the Philosophy of History*,[4] Hegel gives the philosophically untutored reader every encouragement to think that it is possible, without close study of his philosophy as a whole, to catch at least his main drift. What follows—in many respects an oversimplified account—is based almost entirely upon what he has to say in this work. This will be sufficient, at least, to highlight some of the chief differences (and also certain similarities) between his approach and those to be examined in subsequent chapters.

Spirit and freedom   For Hegel, the task of the speculative philosopher of history is shortly stated. It is to elicit the "rationality" of what has occurred—a doctrine he expresses, characteristically, by saying that what philosophy brings to the study of history is the concept of "reason": the belief that "reason is sovereign of the world; that the world, therefore, presents us with a rational process" (p. 9). If we are to follow his own demonstration, however, it is essential, Hegel tells us, that we avoid two possible misunderstandings of what is to be meant by "reason" in this connection.

The first is the sense in which the scientist finds reason in nature. It was in this sense that the Greek philosopher, Anaxagoras, also asserted the formula, "Reason rules the world"; for his conception of a rational process was one which was "in accordance with universal, unchanging laws" (p. 11). But this, as Hegel puts it, is the rationality of "external" causation; it cannot be an appropriate sense for a philosophical account of history, since history is concerned, not with nature, but with the life of spiritual beings. For this reason, a second interpretation, the religious notion of a process controlled by a divine providence, may appear more satisfactory. The rationality of history would then be discovered, not in mere orderliness, but in the realization of a purpose or plan. But the very concept of "providence," Hegel observes, implies that the plan of history is at least partially "concealed from our view" (p. 13); indeed, it is usually considered, by those who use it, to be somewhat presumptuous to inquire too closely into such a plan. Except in some very vague and philosophically uninteresting sense,

---

[4] The account that follows is drawn from the Sibree translation. Page references in the text are to the edition edited by C. J. Friedrich (New York: Dover Publications, Inc., 1956). A good alternative translation of Hegel's Introduction is that by R. S. Hartman, published under the title *Reason in History* (Indianapolis: Bobbs-Merrill Company, Inc., 1953; a Liberal Arts book).

therefore, reference to a plan of providence does not *explain* what goes on in history; it does not *display* its rationality.

A properly philosophical account of history must discover reason actually *operating* in the course of events; it must make clear both *what* is being achieved and *how* it is brought about. A hint, at any rate, as to the first of these can be derived from the fact, already noted, that in some sense history concerns the life of "spirit." For according to Hegel, metaphysical reflection upon the nature of spirit, by contrast with its opposite, matter, shows that the essential characteristic of spirit is self-movement, or "freedom." It is through this that all other, more determinate, spiritual characteristics gain existence. Such reflection also shows that spirituality has many grades or levels, and that freedom, too, is a matter of degree. What we may expect to find in history, therefore, is how human spirituality has developed, how "spirit" has emerged by stages out of "nature." And we may expect this development to show itself as a progressive achievement of human freedom. It is Hegel's claim that when we survey the facts of history "reflectively," this is exactly what we do find. The full realization of a "potential" freedom may thus be regarded as the "aim" of history and "the final cause of the World at large" (p. 19).

But how is such a goal achieved? According to Hegel it is by means of "will"—the only way anything spiritual can be achieved. But although he is insistent that what happens in history is brought about by the wills of individual human beings, he repudiates any notion that freedom might have been won *deliberately*. Men do not normally aim at spiritual development, their own or other people's. Enlightened and virtuous actions do occur; but they are "insignificant on history's broad canvas." What we find rather is "a drama of passions and needs," a welter of "private aims and selfish desires"—nothing that looks like a rational purposive process at all. On the face of it, history is the "slaughter-bench at which the happiness of peoples, the wisdom of states, and the virtue of individuals have been victimized" (p. 21); and any account of the meaning of history must find room for such facts. This Hegel proceeds to do by representing the self-regarding, destructive passions of men as the unconscious "efficient cause" of their own opposite. It is the "cunning of reason," he says, that "it sets the passions to work for itself" (p. 33). Men move toward a rational goal in spite of themselves; their actions are "the means and instruments of a higher and broader purpose of which they know nothing" (p. 25). This is true, furthermore, not only of the masses of the people, but even of those great men or World Historical Individuals, who, according to Hegel, play a crucial role in the process. For these "heroes" of history, although in a sense having "insight into the requirements of the time" (p. 30), do not understand the larger significance of their own actions. They too pursue their own private goals, which simply *coincide* with what is required for the development of freedom. Thus Caesar rescued the Romans from the burden of Senatorial faction; but what he was really aiming at was "the maintenance of his own position, honor, and safety" (p. 29).

As long as we keep our eye on individuals, in fact, we shall never see clearly how "reason rules the world." This is not only because even the great men of history contribute to the development of the human spirit chiefly by the unintended results of their actions. It is also because freedom itself is not conceived by Hegel as the mere expression of individual caprice. True freedom, he says, in typical idealist fashion, is possible only through "discipline"; it is attainable only in an organized society under law. The free and noble savage is not just a myth; he is an absurdity. The social nexus which men require in order to realize their freedom Hegel calls the "state," although this comprises so much more than the purely political arrangements of a community that some broader term like "national culture" might better convey his meaning. The Hegelian state is "the basis and center of the other concrete elements of the life of a people—of Art, of Law, of Morals, of Religion, of Science" (p. 49). It is the "Moral Whole"; the "Reality of Freedom"; the "Objectivity of Spirit"; the "Divine Idea as it exists on Earth" (pp. 38-39).

As the locus of freedom, the state or national culture is the true "historical individual," the proper object of study for the philosophy of history. Hegel would argue, in fact, that before the organization of states, there is no history, properly speaking (a limitation of scope, it might be noted, which seems to be recognized by historians themselves). The philosophical importance of a state depends upon the form (and level) of spirituality which it attains. This is expressible in terms of some general principle or idea which manifests itself in every aspect of the culture, indeed "in all its particular affairs—its wars, institutions, etc." For the understanding of the principle of a culture, Hegel adds, no element is more significant than its religion, "the sphere in which a nation gives itself the definition of that which it regards as the True." The state could even be said to be *based* on religion, for "the concept of God . . . constitutes the general basis of a people's character" (p. 50). According to Hegel, an ordering of at least the more prominent states by reference to the spiritual level of their national principles will be found to correspond with the temporal order of their appearance in world history. The careers of these World Historical Peoples can thus be represented as stages in a single historical development: the rise of the human spirit, which is at the same time the progressive social organization of freedom. In outline at least, Hegel goes on to write the history of the world from this point of view.

The course of World History   So considered, World History falls into four main stages, each with three substages, the center of interest shifting gradually from East to West. It begins with the Oriental societies of the Chinese, Indians, and Persians, continues with those of the Greeks and the Romans, and culminates in the Christian culture of the Germanic nations of Western Europe.

Of the three Oriental nations, Hegel scarcely regards the first two as achieving the status of World Historical Peoples at all. Ancient China was a "theocratic despotism" (p. 112), in which only the emperor was free; and even his freedom, being capricious, was of a low order. The spirit of the society was, at best, that of the family; its members had the status, not of citizens, but of children. According to Hegel, an absence of spontaneity and self-consciousness pervaded every aspect of Chinese culture: its ethics was a collection of fixed rules without rationale; its history consisted of an unreflective recital of discrete facts; its science was a mere collection of techniques. Even more significantly, its laws were regarded as an "external" force by those who obeyed them, almost as if they were laws of nature rather than expressions of human reason and will. Despotism was therefore the form of government *appropriate* to the spirit of the people. By contrast with this monolithic Chinese state, Hegel sees Indian society as, in some respects, spiritually more advanced. For here, at least, can be found a wealth of social diversity. This diversity, however, had a basis, not in any spontaneity of spirit, but in a distinction of nature: the rigid system of castes. To this Hegel attributes a social morality which encouraged the rankest inhumanity, and a religious ideal of escape from the social condition altogether.

Both China and India, on Hegel's account, were static. They had no basis for spiritual development in them, and they have remained in their original condition to his own day. The Persians were the first true World Historical People, their state being the first to "pass away." There is historical evidence of their higher status in the fact that the Persian Empire consisted of a number of component nations, each of which retained its own cultural individuality. Indeed, the laws of the Persians deliberately protected local idiosyncrasies, as it was the good fortune of the Jews to discover. The ruler, furthermore, was not a despot; his power was "regulated by the same principle of law as the obedience of the subject" (p. 114). According to Hegel, the spiritual condition of the Persians is well symbolized by their religion: the worship of Light. As a *natural* symbol of spirit, this was inferior to the frankly anthropomorphic religious conceptions of their World Historical successors, the Greeks. Yet it did, at least, avoid confusing the spiritual with the crassly material. And it reflected the principle of the imperial organization, which, in its relation to the subject peoples, was like an illumination, "imparting to each object a peculiar vitality" (p. 187).

With the Greeks, whose career constitutes the second main stage of world history, there is a breakthrough to a joyous, unreflective individuality of spirit which finds appropriate expression in the pure political democracy of the small city-state. Hegel writes lovingly of the "youthful freshness" and "vitality" of the Greek spirit. Of this, he says, Achilles and Alexander are symbols: the "ideal youths," respectively of poetry and of reality (p. 223). The clash between Greece and Persia issued in a series of World Historical victories at Salamis, Marathon, and Plataea for the materially weaker, but spiritually more highly developed, society. There followed a great but short flowering of Greek culture, the very virtues of its individuality eventually bringing about its decline through factional strife within the city-states and incessant wars between them (the one between Athens and Sparta being the best known and the most disastrous). According to Hegel, the "principle of corruption" was "reflection" (p. 267). This gradually destroyed the "customary" basis of Greek political virtue; and the Athenians were therefore right to regard Socrates, with his questioning, as the enemy of their social order. Attractive as it was, particularly in its artistic achievement, Greek society nevertheless *deserved* to be superseded. For the level of freedom which it realized *depended* upon the institution of slavery. The slaves were not just unfortunate, eliminable exceptions to the Greek concept of man as free.

If the Orient represents the inarticulate childhood of the human spirit, and Greece its poetic adolescence, in Rome we find its prosaic early manhood. The Roman state originated in a contrived union of rootless robber bands, and from the first, its existence had required "the severest discipline and self-sacrifice to the grand object of the union"—every citizen in the early period being a soldier, and the state being frankly based on war (p. 284). The Roman principle of positive law, together with its associated concept of a strictly defined legal right, was antithetical to that of the Greeks. Its "abstract" spirituality can be seen also in the harsh, contractual nature of Roman marriage, the unfeeling, imitative character of Roman art, and the lifeless rationalization of the Olympian deities in the Roman pantheon. Yet as an organization of freedom (Hartman's phrase), the Roman state was strong precisely where Greek society was weak; and its "reflective" solution of the problem of freedom must be counted a spiritual advance. Up to the Second Punic War the Roman spirit was in a period of gestation. Thereafter, with the cessation of the early disputes between patricians and plebs, it imposed its principle upon the world in a period of workmanlike expansion. It was during this, the second stage of their history, that the Romans contacted their World Historical predecessors, the Greeks—the same stage at which the Greeks had contacted the Persians. Only after world domination had been achieved did the corruption of absolute power result in the downfall of the Republic. The subsequent reconstitution of the state as the Empire produced no more than a caricature of the ancient Roman spirit. Its main significance for World History lies in the contact which it ensured with the Germanic nations of the north, and the opportunity it provided for the spread of the Christian religion, which was to provide the principle of the next World Historical People.

With the Germanic World, the human spirit reaches its full maturity. For, according to Hegel, Christianity, which was adopted by the barbarians who overran the Roman Empire, perfectly expresses the principle that man as such is free. And although it has taken some eight centuries for this notion to gain concrete expression in the institutions of Western society, Hegel regards the constitutional regimes of his own day as approximating closely to the requirements of a Christian commonwealth. The "first consolidation of Christianity into a political form" was attempted by Charlemagne at the close of the earliest period of Western history (p. 365). This, however, proved abortive, and it was followed by a "terrible discipline of culture" (p. 344)—the social chaos of feudalism in the Middle Ages, and the corruption of the Church, which, while seeking to become a secular power, neglected the task of translating its spiritual message into concrete social terms. With the rise of monarchy in the fifteenth century and the Protestant Reformation in the sixteenth, Hegel sees men beginning to face more squarely the problem of "building up the edifice of secular relations" in accordance with the spirit of Christianity (p. 422). In spite of his notoriously good opinion of the Prussian state, however, he is under no illusion that this task has been completed. His account thus stops abruptly with the remark: "This is the point which spirit has attained" (p. 456).

Dialectic and necessity Hegel's account of World History is an expansion of his oft-quoted remark: "the Eastern nations knew only that *one* is free; the Greek and Roman world only that *some* are free; while *we* know that all men absolutely (man *as man*) are free" (p. 19). In calling history a "rational process," however, he clearly intends more than the simple claim that its course has in fact been in this gratifying direction. For Hegel, the rationality of history is shown also in the *way* that goal has been reached: in the kind of *order* displayed by the successive stages of the process. Each World Historical People, as we have seen, makes its contribution to spiritual advance through the development and cultural assertion of its own distinctive idea or principle. It is Hegel's claim that these principles are related in such a way that they represent a "logical" progression. By this he does not mean that they follow from each other in accordance with the rules of formal logic (which he tends to regard as expressing a rather stilted and elementary form of rationality). It is rather that they have the kind of order which he believes can be found in the stages of any constructive piece of rational reflection which proceeds from an inadequate, one-sided understanding of its object to an ever more sophisticated, many-sided grasp of it. Such an order Hegel calls "dialectical" (p. 63).

The Hegelian theory of dialectic (of which only the sketchiest indication is possible here) is given in its most highly developed and technical form in a work entitled *Science of Logic*, where pure concepts are represented as giving rise to each other through an orderly three-stage process of development. The inadequacies of an original concept, or "thesis," drive us into asserting its "antithesis," the tension between them eventually being resolved through a third concept which effects a "synthesis" of the preceding elements—this process being repeated as each synthesis, with further reflection, becomes the thesis of a new and "higher" triad. Hegel regards such a pattern of tension and resolution as the very "mechanism" of reason; and this is what he claims to discover, although in a much less definite form, in the rational progress of history. According to Hegel, at the most general level of description, history displays a "dialectic of national principles." The principles of Greece and Rome, for example, are seen as antithetical ways of trying to express the idea of freedom in society, the latter being a reaction against the one-sidedness of the former. The Germanic State is a concrete synthesis of the free individuality of the Greeks and the abstract legalism of the Romans. Hegel also finds a social dialectic at more detailed levels of the histories of his World Historical Peoples. Exhibiting it, he claims, provides a "deeper" understanding of historical movement than could be given by any merely causal analysis.

In view of the use to which many Marxists have put it, Hegel's notion of a historical dialectic is bound to raise the question of the extent to which his theory of historical change is deterministic. Sidney Hook has called it "the most influential of all social determinisms." [5] And Hegel certainly did assert the "necessity" of many historical events which he regarded as crucial for the dialectical progress of history. The rise of Caesar to the supreme power in Rome, he says, "must not be regarded as a thing of chance; for it was *necessary*—postulated by the circumstances." Similar statements could be cited regarding such apparently incommensurable events as the defeat of the Persian Empire and the death of Alexander while still a youth (pp. 221, 273).

Yet it is notable (in spite of what Gardiner says about dialectical "prophecies") that Hegel never claims that a philosophical grasp of history's necessity enables us to predict its course. He does say that some further development of spirit might be looked for in America, once it achieves cultural independence from Europe; but he refuses to speculate on the form this development might take. Even with regard to events now past, Hegel does not really attempt to show that each follows inevitably from what preceded it in the main line of historical development. Indeed, when he writes about the victories of the Greeks, it is almost with bated breath: "the interest of the World's History hung trembling in the balance" (p. 257). What he says about the contribution of great individuals, too, suggests that the notion of *contingency*— the fortunate timely availability of both men and conditions—bulks large in his account. There is no indication, for example, that he thought Alexander, Caesar, or Napoleon to be "replaceable," as Engels was later to say that all great men are. Hegel did deny that these could accomplish anything for which the time was not "ripe"; but he envisaged their unpredictable interventions as making a real difference to the course of history.

[5] *The Hero in History* (New York: The John Day Company, Inc., 1943), p. 60.

What then does he mean by historical necessity? Let us look further at what he says about the rise of Caesar being "postulated by the circumstances."

> The Republic could no longer exist in Rome. We see, especially from Cicero's writings, how all public affairs were decided by the private authority of the more eminent citizens—by their power, their wealth; and what tumultuary proceedings marked all political transactions. In the Republic, therefore, there was no longer any security; that could be looked for only in a single will. . . . Caesar, judged by the great scope of history, did the Right; since he furnished a mediating element, and that kind of political bond which men's condition required [p. 312].

If the necessity of the predictable enters here at all, it is at any rate not the rise of Caesar that is necessary in this sense. Conditions being what they were, Hegel claims, the Republic *would* necessarily fall. But would the state be saved? Only if there was a Caesar to do what was required—and if he would do it. What was required was, of course, "necessary"; but only in the sense of being necessary *for* the salvation of the state—and for the continued development of history in the direction of increasing freedom. The latter is something which, in Hegel's account, is never guaranteed. There are in fact periods in history when "the whole enormous gain of previous culture appears to have been entirely lost; after which, unhappily, a new commencement has been necessary" (p. 56).

If the necessity which Hegel attributes to history is of this non-deterministic kind, however, the philosophical understanding he claims to gain through discovering a dialectical progression in history begins to take on a certain resemblance to the rational understanding discussed in Chapter 2 of this book. Given a certain original state of affairs (the primitive spirituality of the Orient) and a purpose or goal to be achieved (the level of spiritual freedom of Hegel's own society), we can understand each step in the dialectical movement from one to the other as a step there was *reason for taking*. If the level of Germanic spirituality was to be attained, the free self-expression of the Greeks was *needed* as a reaction against the "substantial" morality of the Orientals; the "abstract" legal freedom of the Romans was *needed* as a reaction against the unreflective irresponsibility of the Greeks; the concrete social organization of the Germans was *needed* in order to consolidate the spiritual gains of both these earlier stages. What was previously referred to as "rational explanation" thus seems to be at least one element in the Hegelian dialectic of history. The novelty is Hegel's conviction that a rational progress must pass through and "overcome" every relevant form of "error" in its zig-zag course toward "truth." The step there is reason for taking may thus often not *appear* to be a step toward the goal—as the Dark Ages, for example, may not *appear* to be an advance over the civilization of Rome.

If the foregoing is a fair sketch of at least some of Hegel's chief contentions about history, what are we to say of the objection most often leveled against him as a "metaphysical" theorist: that the Hegelian system is spun out of its author's imagination a priori: that, in bringing to the study of history the alleged speculative knowledge that "reason rules the world," it makes an illegitimate rationalist assumption that the actual course of events must conform to the reasonings of the philosopher? W. H. Walsh formulates the objection thus: Contrary to what some critics seem to have believed, Hegel does not "deduce the details of history" from a set of logical abstractions. He does, however, claim to be able to derive "its outline or skeleton plot" from "purely philosophical premises." Thus he claims to know a priori "that history must be the gradual realization of freedom; he even knows that this process must complete itself in four distinct stages." Walsh concludes: "If this is not determining the course of history apart from experience, it is hard to know what is." [6]

Now it cannot be denied that Hegel claims to know some such general truths about history independently of the survey he presents in his *Lectures*. One can see, perhaps, why he would have claimed that they could be proved "philosophically." If history is by definition about the development of spirit, and if philosophical analysis shows the concepts of spirit and freedom to be necessarily connected, then it would appear to follow that the theme of history will concern the development of freedom. If a spiritual development, furthermore, can only be achieved by a series of dialectically related steps (which Hegel would certainly claim to know by "speculative cognition"), then it would appear to follow, too, that dialectical steps leading to the grade of spirituality actually existing must have been taken at some previous times and places. And if a dialectical order is the one in which rational reflection would progress through the elements of an idea to its "synthesis," and this order is determinate, then it might also be argued that a philosophical analysis of the "idea" expressed in an existing culture will reveal both the necessary elements which must previously have gained expression, and the order in which they were expressed. The claim to know all this, it should be remarked, does not quite amount to claiming knowledge of the course of history on the basis of "purely philosophical premises"; for the Hegelian philosopher cannot say anything about history's *actual* course unless he knows first what stage of spirituality has been reached. Nor does it entail the predictability of history. What it entails is the *retrodictability* of the necessary conditions of what has actually been found to exist, in accordance with a metaphysical theory. This claim for "speculative cognition," however, is startling enough. And, from the standpoint of the ordinary historian, at any rate, it would surely count as "determining the course of history apart from experience."

[6] *Philosophy of History: An Introduction*, p. 151.

Yet it remains difficult to say, without extended further consideration of Hegel's system as a whole, just how damaging the charge of
a priorism is. For "speculative cognition," as Hegel understands it, is
not logical deduction from first principles known intuitively; he is not
that kind of a metaphysical rationalist. His whole philosophy arises out
of reflection on "experience," including *historical* experience. Thus what
philosophy "brings to the study of history" may be no more than it owes.
Fortunately, we are not obliged either to assess Hegel's speculative
proofs or to accept on faith his own claim that they could be produced.
For Hegel himself offers us quite another route into his philosophy of
history. In a passage in which, significantly, he comments adversely upon
the a prioristic tendencies of his own countrymen, he says that although
the rationality of history is known to him in advance, he is content that
for his readers this should be a "hypothesis" or "inference." And he
adds: "We must proceed historically—empirically" (p. 10). As Herbert
Marcuse has observed, this may appear "an odd approach for an idealis-
tic philosophy of history." [7] Yet it certainly seems to promise something
like *empirical* verification of a *metaphysical* hypothesis about the course
of history.

In combating objections to his so-called "a priori method," Hegel
in fact goes so far as to compare his own procedure with that of a
natural scientist, who must also "insinuate ideas into the empirical
data" (p. 64). If we are going to be able to recognize the manifestations of spirit in history, Hegel insists, we need

> not only a disciplined faculty of abstraction, but an intimate ac-
> quaintance with the Idea. The investigator must be familiar *a priori*
> (if we like to call it so), with the whole circle of conceptions to which
> the principles in question belong—just as Kepler . . . must have been
> familiar *a priori* with ellipses, with cubes and squares, and with ideas
> of their relations, before he could discover, from the empirical data,
> those immortal "Laws" of his, which are none other than forms of
> thought pertaining to those classes of conceptions.

The chief difference between the natural scientist and the philosophical
historian, in this connection, is that history "does not proceed according
to the categories of Understanding [i. e., those of scientific thought],
but according to the categories of *Reason*," of which the concept of a
dialectically developing freedom is the chief. In terms of the kind of
understanding they seek, in other words, the two approaches are different. But this should not obscure the fact that *both* methods involve
a priori and empirical elements.

The principle   Even if Hegel offers something approaching empirical demonstra-
of selection   tion of his conclusions, however, there arises, for many critics, an-
                    other difficulty about the basis on which he asserts them. For even
if all the details of the alleged Hegelian pattern could be vouched for by

---

[7] *Reason and Revolution*, 2nd ed. (New York: Humanities Press, 1954), p. 225.

historians, they may appear, when taken together, to constitute a ludicrously thin account of World History. As Bertrand Russell observes, it is odd, surely, that what is important takes place around the Mediterranean.[8] Pursuing a similar line of criticism, Mandelbaum objects to Hegel's neglect of primitive societies—the whole of Africa being "unhistorical" for him—and to his bringing in each of his World Historical Peoples only once, thus implying that the ancient Greeks, but not the modern, were historical, and that nothing of significance has happened in China for 4,000 years.[9] Worse still, even cultures which Hegel himself admits to be quite advanced are often relegated to the sidelines of history: they are excluded from the main movement in terms of which its meaning is to be read. The only role found for the Mohammedan World, for example, is that of providing a stimulus to Germanic unity (the Crusades were "the Trojan War of Christendom" [p. 231]); and he finds no role for the Slavic nations at all. Hegel's "verification" of his metaphysical hypothesis thus easily takes on the appearance of an all too convenient selection from the welter of historical facts. As Mandelbaum puts it, "what facts are significant becomes a question of what facts confirm the hypothesis."

Now it is difficult to deny that Hegel's selection of historical details—in themselves, at times, somewhat fanciful—often looks like special pleading. In establishing the principle or idea which determines the role to be assigned to a culture, for example, Hegel generally seems much more concerned about what might *confirm* the spiritual grade he assigns it than about what might count *against* this. Yet Mandelbaum's attack on the excessive "selectivity" of his account—as if in limiting himself to tracing the single-track linear development he does, he offends against some ideal of "comprehensiveness"—appears to have the mark of misunderstanding in it. For Hegel makes it clear that he is not writing "universal history" in an ordinary sense; his Introduction deliberately distinguishes between "universal" and "philosophical" history (p. 4). To revert to the analysis of Chapter 3 for a moment: universal history is "descriptive"; and even then, it is of the "period" rather than the "theme" variety. Thus the question whether every occurrence of a certain standard of intrinsic importance has been included is a relevant one for it. Hegel's philosophical history, by contrast, is "explanatory" (p. 13); and it has, according to him, a quite specific historical eventuality to explain: the alleged spiritual achievement represented by the Germanic State. What goes into Hegel's account, therefore, is, and surely should be, limited to what contributed to this achievement. To quarrel with the exclusion of Chinese, Arabs, and primitive African tribes is thus to quarrel—and in most cases with little

---

[8] *History of Western Philosophy* (New York: Simon and Schuster, Inc., 1946), p. 762.

[9] "Can There Be a Philosophy of History?" *American Scholar*, IX, No. 1 (1939-40), 79.

historical plausibility—with Hegel's judgment as to the extent of their contribution.

One could, of course, quarrel with the general content of Hegel's philosophical history on other grounds. It might be objected, for example, that the analysis he offers of the "spirit" of the cultures he does include is simply incorrect, so that his claim to have traced the route of spiritual accumulation which ends in his own society in fact fails. Or it might be questioned whether the Germanic State really represents the highest level of the organization of freedom attained by men, and thus whether it represents a proper terminus for a Hegelian-style philosophical history at all. Even more radically, the whole Hegelian analysis of spirituality might be questioned, together with the implication that the social organization of freedom is the most important thing that can happen in human history: in other words, the whole metaphysical and ethical basis of Hegel's selection of a *theme* for philosophical history could be denied. What is illegitimate is to criticize Hegel's account without reference either to the alleged *philosophical* inadequacy of the author's selection of a theme, or the alleged *historical* inadequacy of his elaboration of it. As for the fact that the theater of history borders the Mediterranean: Hegel himself offers a fairly conventional environmental explanation of that. In a long section entitled "The Geographical Basis of History" he argues that certain kinds of environment inhibit spiritual development. This, incidentally, is quite consistent with the spiritualistic indeterminism attributed to him previously. For he clearly does not claim that other kinds of environment "produce" such development.

Metaphysical explanation We have noted two sorts of objections to Hegel's theory which center on its relation to his whole metaphysical position: that the latter provides him with independent a priori "proofs" of his claims about history, and that it provides him with a principle of selection which allows him to ignore whatever he finds inconvenient. There is, however, a third and much more radical sense in which the Hegelian account has often been rejected as "too metaphysical." This can be shown if we revert to what was said earlier about the likeness between the dialectical necessities of Hegel's philosophical history and the rational explanations of ordinary historians.

When a historian explains by reference to "reasons," what he explains is the actions of individual human agents. Such explanation requires the attribution of appropriate purposes, knowledge, and intentions to the agents concerned, not only for its truth but for its very *intelligibility*. Hegel begins by claiming that history is made by men; that individual human wills are the "efficient causes" of historical change. He goes on, however, to make it clear that the purpose or goal in terms of which the philosopher is to discern the rationality of history is not that of the individuals who jointly take the dialectically necessary steps; it is not the purpose even of World Historical Individuals. Nor does any individual have the knowledge of the situation required to represent the next step as the one to take; or intend the taking of that step *as such* when the step is in fact taken. The urge to find an agent for all these unclaimed purposes, beliefs, and intentions, if they are to perform an explanatory function, is understandably strong. It is hardly surprising, therefore, to find Hegel eventually talking as if "Spirit" itself were such an agent. It is "Spirit," he says, which "uses" the passions of individuals for a higher purpose; it is "Spirit" which "assumes" the form of the State; it is "Spirit" which, in the course of the dialectic, is "at war with itself"; it is "Spirit" which has the development of freedom as its "absolute aim" (pp. 25, 17, 55, 37). In the end, indeed, history is represented as "the biography of the World Spirit"; its rationality, and also its ultimate meaning, are to be found in its being the process through which the World Spirit "develops itself." Thus, although the *form* of explanation offered by Hegel is of a type familiar to ordinary historical thinking, its *content* makes it thoroughly metaphysical.

Most contemporary philosophers of history, including many who would repudiate the label "positivist," would flatly deny the legitimacy of concepts like the Hegelian "World Spirit." Before dismissing it summarily, however, it is salutary to remember just how far historians themselves are often prepared to go in Hegel's direction. As Herbert Butterfield has put it, history *does*, to a large extent, go on "over our heads"; [10] and we *can* often organize the facts of history, as Hegel says we should, in terms of ideas which were not the ideas of the individual agents concerned. We may not approve of the personification of "Spirit" as a way of putting those ideas to work in explanations. But when historians speak of the "Renaissance Spirit" or the "Spirit of Puritanism" manifesting itself in various occurrences and conditions, they use the word "spirit" in a sense approaching Hegel's. Should we not be willing, then, when the history of the world is our theme, to speak of the manifestations of the "Human Spirit"? Can we not sensibly say, at least, that history develops *as if* the Human Spirit were developing itself by a series of rationally connectible steps? This sort of reflection often issues in a limited defense of metaphysical approaches in philosophy of history along pragmatic lines. According to Patrick Gardiner, for example, it is characteristic of metaphysics generally to put old terms to new uses, and by stretching their meanings, to suggest "fresh ways of describing and ordering the material." He cites Hegel's use of the word "principle" as an example of this. [11]

Such a defense would obviously not satisfy Hegel. He would not regard his claim that Spirit develops itself in history as just a "convenient way of talking" about the actual direction taken by the unintended results of human actions. For him, "Spirit" is no mere

[10] *Christianity and History* (New York: Charles Scribner's Sons, 1949), p. 94.
[11] "Metaphysics and History," in *The Nature of Metaphysics*, ed. David Pears (New York: St. Martin's Press, Inc., 1957), p. 97.

"organizing" or "colligating" concept; it is used to assert a *metaphysical explanation* of the course of events. Not that he quite conceives of Spirit as an additional Agent working alongside human individuals, trying to manipulate and motivate them as they do each other. The Hegelian World Spirit is *immanent* in history; it is nothing apart from the actions of individuals which unconsciously express its "activity" of self-development. The case for at least considering such a claim would have been stronger had Hegel offered some more general account of the way individual actions come to "express" the purposive activity of the World Spirit. What we should like to see is how human actions, in their very nature, although unknowingly, bring about what is needed for the further development of human spirituality as a whole. Hegel does show in specific cases how the aims and conceptions of individuals and peoples coincided with what was in this sense "historically required." But he does not show *in general* that the passions of individuals are such as to bring about a situation in which there can be a "dialectic of national principles." The Hegelian account of history recognizes two levels at which the course of events can be described, each with its own kind of mechanism. The two levels, however, never really mesh.

AN EMPIRICAL APPROACH

7

A. J. Toynbee   To turn from the system of Hegel to that of Toynbee is to turn from the formidable argumentation of a professional—indeed somewhat professorial—philosopher to the diffuse and often highly personal reflections of a literary historian who would himself make no claim to be called a philosopher at all. It is also to turn from a perceptive, but to modern eyes somewhat amateurish, sketch of history offered as a rough exemplification of a metaphysical thesis, to an attempt, supposedly without preconceptions, to take the measure of universal history through an almost incredible mastery of its details. What Toynbee has to say about history requires ten fat volumes, which appeared in three stages over a twenty-year period, under the title, A *Study of History*.[1] Fortunately, a more convenient approach to his work exists in the form of a two-volume abridgment by D. C. Somervell. The chief disadvantage of the latter (although not, perhaps, for present purposes) is that it necessarily cuts away what critics and supporters alike have often regarded as one of Toynbee's chief attractions: his long, purely historical digressions.

Estimates of Toynbee's work have varied widely. "Have you seen what they're saying about Arnold Toynbee?" asks a *New York Times* advertisement of 1955: "Amazing . . . an immortal masterpiece . . . the greatest work of our time. . . ." Even an ultimately hostile critic like the Dutch historian Pieter Geyl feels constrained to remark: "what flashes of insight, what instructive juxtapositions. . . . what learning, what

---

[1] (New York: Oxford University Press, 1934-54). Page references in the text are to the volumes of this edition, which is now available in paperback. Two further volumes, the last entitled *Reconsiderations*, are not taken into account in the outline of Toynbee's theory presented here.

brilliance!" [2] More typical of the views of the academic community, perhaps, is this comment: "A *Study of History* presents an enormous mass of historical material, strung along a thin line of argument, often represented only by a single word, generally Greek." [3] Nor have serious critics always been willing to admit that Toynbee presents an *argument* at all. By even friendly ones he has regularly been excused as a poet, prophet, or mystic more often than taken seriously as what he claims to be: a historian, by historical and scientific methods, discerning the pattern and significance of the whole human past. In some, it might be added, he has aroused more than purely professional, more than narrowly intellectual, resistance. Of Toynbee's work, the English historian, Hugh Trevor-Roper, writes: "I find it not merely erroneous . . . but hateful." [4] And a similiar emotional reaction expresses itself in Ceyl's final judgment that Toynbee's conclusions constitute "a blasphemy against Western civilization." [5]

The unit of historical study   The declared aim of Toynbee's *Study*, at any rate as it was originally conceived, was to compare all the civilizations known to man in order to discover the causes of their rise and fall. Toynbee tells us that the stimulus to such an inquiry came to him in a flash of insight in the period immediately prior to World War I, when, as a teacher of ancient history at Oxford, he suddenly found himself reading Thucydides' *History of the Peloponnesian War* with new eyes: the eyes of one undergoing a similar experience. The affinity he henceforth felt with the Greeks of the fifth century B.C.—by contrast, for example, with his own European forebears of the Middle Ages—led him to undertake a comprehensive comparative study. This, he hoped, might eventually justify a prediction of the fate of a Western Civilization already experiencing a "Time of Troubles."

From the first, Toynbee linked the pursuit of this professionally unusual goal with an attack on his fellow historians for what he called their "parochial," meaning essentially national, historical interests. He justified the shift of scale in his own inquiry by claiming that only at the level of a whole civilization can the events of national histories become really intelligible. Thus the history of Great Britain cannot be written without constant reference to what is going on in Continental Europe. The intelligible field for the English historian is, in fact, Western Christendom (I, 17ff). Applying the same criterion to all existing political entities, Toynbee arrived at a list of contemporary civilizations which includes (besides the Western) the Orthodox Christian, the Islamic, the Hindu, and the Far Eastern—the latter being sub-

---

[2] *Debates with Historians* (Cleveland, Ohio: World Publishing Co., 1958; a Meridian book), p. 158.
[3] H. N. Frye, "Toynbee and Spengler," *The Canadian Forum*, XXVII, No. 319 (August, 1947), 111.
[4] "Arnold Toynbee's Millennium," *Encounter*, VIII, No. 6 (June, 1957), 26.
[5] *Debates with Historians*, p. 178.

divided into Chinese and Japanese-Korean branches. Further civilizations, now extinct, were discovered by tracing each of these living
examples back to its origins. Behind the Western, for example, is its
parent, the Greco-Roman civilization, which Toynbee calls Hellenic;
behind the Islamic is the Syriac, a society familiar to most of us through
our reading of the Bible; and so on. Behind this earlier group as a whole
lies a still more ancient group, beyond which Toynbee could find only
primitive societies. In all, he discovered twenty-one (sometimes ex-
panded to twenty-three) fully developed civilizations, divisible into
three "generations," through the period of some 6,000 years since the
"cake of custom" of primitive man was first broken and civilized man
appeared on the scene.[6]

Having identified the subject of his inquiry, Toynbee raises the
first of four large questions which will guide his work through the first
six volumes: the question "How do civilizations arise?" Primitive societies are static; civilizations are in constant process of development.
Two common explanations, racial and environmental, are proposed only
to be rejected on the empirical ground that they not only fail to
explain all the actual cases, but also fail to explain why, in identical conditions, civilizations sometimes do and sometimes do not arise. Toynbee finds a "clue" to the mystery of origins in the collection of myths
in which the spiritual experiences of men have been enshrined. The
hypothesis he derives from this source is that creative activity is found
only in a situation in which, because of its difficulty, men are roused
to some unprecedented effort. The formula in which he expresses this
idea is "challenge-and-response" (I, 271ff).

By following up his "mythological clue," Toynbee finds the origins
of first generation civilizations in responses to a variety of challenges
offered by the physical environment; and he is thus enabled to deny that
civilizations arise naturally out of especially favorable conditions. The
Egyptiac civilization, for example, originated in the lower Nile valley
when, faced by the progressive desiccation of the African grasslands, a
primitive society, instead of moving south and keeping its way of life
intact, set to work to drain the valley marshes. The Sumeric civilization
originated in similar fashion in the valley of the Tigris and Euphrates.
The Mayan and Andean civilizations in America responded to the challenge of the tropical forest and the bleak coastal plateau, respectively;
the Minoan civilization, centered on the island of Crete, responded to
the challenge of the sea. The challenges which explain the rise of second
and third generations were presented less by physical nature than by
the human environment—the "interregnum" of social chaos that followed the breakdown and disintegration of their predecessors. But the
explanatory formula of challenge-and-response still applies.

To make the formula more precise, Toynbee offers a series of what
he calls "comparisons in three terms" (II, 290). It would be naïve, he

---

[6] This scheme is considerably modified in Toynbee's *Reconsiderations*.

says, to jump to the conclusion that the sterner the challenge, the finer would be the response. A challenge may in some cases be so severe that a successful response becomes impossible; it can be so weak that it provokes no response at all. Thus Massachusetts presented European colonists with a more severe challenge than Dixie, and evoked from them a much more powerful response; but the still less favorable conditions of Labrador proved altogether too much. In a section entitled "The Golden Mean," Toynbee argues that civilizations are responses to *mean* or *optimum* challenges. In applying this notion, he discovers a number of societies which, in the face of an unduly strong challenge, almost, but not quite, made a successful response. Examples of these "abortive" civilizations are the Vikings, who collapsed in the face of the severe natural challenge of Iceland and Greenland, and the Celtic Christians of the Far Western Fringe, who were similarly overpowered by the *human* challenge of a neighboring Western Civilization in an expansive phase (II, 322ff).

The rise and fall of civilizations

Having given an account of the origins of civilizations, Toynbee passes to his second question: "How do civilizations grow?" Basically, this question receives the same answer as the first. They grow by responding to a *series* of challenges. But Toynbee's description of the creative movement now becomes more complicated. There is a hint of social dialectic in his suggestion that an optimum response is one which, rather than leaving a society in equilibrium, raises further problems, thus encouraging continuity of development. It is made clear, too, that an important distinction needs to be drawn between those creative individuals and minority groups who originate responses, and the uncreative majorities they lead. The leadership of a growing society, Toynbee tells us, normally falls to some group which has been prepared for its creative role through an archetypal experience he calls "withdrawal-and-return," and which he goes on to illustrate from a wide range of world literature (III, 248). Under the spell of his favorite philosopher, Henri Bergson, he represents the resulting process of social growth as the expression of a vital *élan* in the society, which manifests itself first in one part and then in another.

But what is the criterion of growth? Not, says Toynbee, any resulting increase of control over the physical environment, expressed in improvements in material techniques. Nor is it an increase in the society's control over its human environment, expressed perhaps in its conquest of neighboring peoples. For improvement in, say, agricultural or industrial techniques often takes place when civilizations are past their peaks; and geographical expansion may be an expression of militarism, which Toynbee later identifies as a symptom of decline. The criterion of growth is to be found rather in a change, with the passage of time, in the *character* of the major challenges facing a society—a change for which Toynbee coins the term "etherialization," and which he finds paralleled in the development of human individuals (III, 174ff). There is a gradual shift from material to more spiritual challenges; from external to internal ones. Thus, in the history of the West, we find an early external challenge in the onslaught of the Scandinavian tribes, to which a civilization, in the early stages of its growth, responded with the feudal system. But the operation of that system itself eventually presented a further—this time more internal—challenge, arising out of the social, economic, and political divisions which it entailed. It became clear that a new relationship between class-divided individuals was needed. The response of Western Civilization was the rise of the sovereign national state.

Examination of the growth process leads Toynbee to the discovery of a further group of civilizations: the "arrested" ones of the Polynesians, Nomads, Esquimaux, Osmanlis, and Spartans. This brings his grand total up to thirty or thirty-three. Unlike the abortive group, these societies did make a successful response to a primary challenge, but to one so severe that the task of maintaining the position thus won absorbed all the society's spiritual resources thereafter. The possibility of such arrests underlines the flexibility of Toynbee's theory of development, which consists in the elaboration of a norm and the description of a series of departures from it. Even among the fully developed civilizations, it might be added, the length, speed, and general character of the growth process exhibit very wide differences. And, as Toynbee explains its nature, the growth of a given civilization could, in theory, go on indefinitely.

It is, however, a melancholy fact that all civilizations (with the possible exception of our own) have stopped growing; they have one and all, at some stage, broken down. The marks of breakdown can be deduced directly from what Toynbee has already said about the nature of social growth. They are a failure of creativity on the part of the leaders, and a gradual, consequent loss of social unity due to the withdrawal of the allegiance of the majority. Toynbee's third question concerns the causes of such states of affairs.

The account he gives of the breakdown of civilizations includes a fascinating study of the psychology of leadership and the limitations of social mimesis, the details of which cannot be gone into here. His most important explanatory concept is that of "the nemesis of creativity" (IV, 245ff): the tendency for the very success of a response, for a number of reasons, to unfit the protagonist for the next challenge that has to be faced. Thus, even during the period of growth, that group in a society which responds successfully to one challenge is seldom the one which responds to the next, so that the leadership must continuously pass from group to group. Breakdown occurs when a minority which, through a failure of creativity, has lost its claim to the mimesis of the society at large, insists nevertheless on imposing its will on it. This change—the most fateful occurrence in the life history of a civilization—Toynbee describes as the transformation of a "creative" into a merely "dominant" minority. The careers of such dominant minorities usually harden into some self-stultifying idolatry: the self-adulation of Athens as "the education of Hellas," for example; the worship of the ghost of a dead Roman Empire by the Byzantine Christians; the total commitment to a successful but restrictive technique, like that of the Spartans. The sin of pride—the loss of a sense of proportion, which Toynbee calls the "intoxication of victory" (IV, 505ff)—is another common spiritual cause of breakdown. This is clearly illustrated, he believes, in the history of the medieval Papacy.

Breakdown is followed by disintegration; and it is to an examination of the nature and the course of this fourth and final phase that Toynbee devotes the largest part of his first six volumes. This is perhaps more appropriate than it may at first sight appear. For it turns out, surprisingly enough, that the disintegration phase of most civilizations constitutes the major portion of their histories.

It has sometimes been asserted that Toynbee's theory of history, which in its account of the first three phases of the life of a civilization was flexible and spiritualistic, suddenly becomes tight and mechanical when it offers us, in the final phase, an inevitable pattern of decay. Yet Toynbee leaves room for considerable variation, even here. Thus a civilization, at a certain point in the disintegration process, may become "petrified," and remain unchanged thereafter for thousands of years— a fate which in fact befell the Egyptiac society of the first generation (V, 2). And even after a civilization has been declared officially dead, remnants may continue to exist as "fossils" in the bodies of its successors (V, 8). Two examples of such fossilized civilizations are the Parsees of India and the Jewish community of the West, both of them deriving originally from the second generation Syriac society. As might be expected, this pigeonholing tour de force has not particularly endeared Toynbee to the subjects of his analysis.

The normal pattern of disintegration consists of a gradual widening of that social schism which originated at the point of breakdown. The society becomes increasingly divided into three main fractions, as the masses, in response to the challenge of their own now dominant minority, secede to form a "proletariat"—which, for Toynbee, includes all those who feel themselves in, but not of, the society (V, 63). This proletariat is itself divided into two groups. The one, the *internal* proletariat, exists within the political boundaries of the disintegrating society. In the case of the Hellenic society, it included, for example, the economically disinherited, the conquered peoples, the victims of the slave trade. The other, the *external* proletariat, is composed of barbarians beyond the frontiers, who were formerly within the growing civilization's range of cultural radiation. Their pressure on the frontiers increases during the disintegration period, until they finally break through and plow the civilization under. In the chaotic interregnum which follows, a new society may come to birth. But it is in the souls of the penalized members of the internal, not the external, proletariat, that the spiritual resources necessary for such new growth are to be found. This process of rebirth expresses itself historically in the rise of a new higher religion. Thus Western Civilization was born out of the "chrysalis" of the Christian Church, itself a creative work of the Roman proletariat.

Long before final dissolution, the dominant minority, the third fraction of the disintegrating society, will also have performed a characteristic work of construction—if not, in Toynbee's view, of "creation." For the "Time of Troubles" which follows social breakdown ends eventually in the establishment of a universal state, usually by a "knockout blow" which terminates a series of fratricidal wars of ever increasing severity. Such a "rally," as Toynbee calls it, no more than delays the final outcome. The normal rhythm of disintegration, he says, has three and a half beats of Rout-Rally-Rout (VI, 284ff). Throughout this period, the uncreative dominant minority is faced by a recurring challenge, which it repeatedly fails to meet. In the case of the Hellenic society, this was the need for some ecumenical form of political organization appropriate to the complex economic system which had replaced the more primitive economic self-sufficiency of the Greek city-states. The first clear sign that the challenge would not be met, in Toynbee's view, was the outbreak of that Peloponnesian War, Thucydides' account of which had first turned his mind to the question of the fate of the West.

The significance of universal churches By the end of his sixth volume, Toynbee's theory of the rise and fall of civilizations is in all essentials complete. If four additional volumes are needed to round it out, one might expect that they would simply present further confirmation of points already made. Toynbee's own explanation of their function hints at something of the kind, but also at something further. For whereas he had, at the beginning, regarded a civilization as alone the intelligible unit of historical study because it formed the area of contact between states, his investigation now shows that this is true only during the first three stages of development. In disintegration, contacts with other societies are common—in addition to which there is, of course, the "apparentation" relation established by the emergence of a new society out of an old. It is thus for further light on universal states and their downfalls, on barbarian heroic ages (known to us in epic poetry), on the rise of universal churches—and, in general, on the various sorts of contacts between civilizations in space and time—that we turn in the later volumes.

In those volumes, we do in fact find all these matters discussed. But we also find a change of emphasis—even a change of doctrine—so striking that some critics have been inclined to regard the later volumes almost as a new work. The big change (although there were anticipations as far back as Vol. I) is in the basic interpretation to be placed on the question "Why do civilizations rise and fall?" As we have ourselves interpreted this question so far, it has meant "What causes them to do so?" But Toynbee now becomes far more interested in an overtly teleological interpretation of the same question: "What is the point of their doing so?" The answer he gives transmutes a sociology of history, in which spiritual endeavor and even organized religion have certainly played a most significant causal role, into a theology of history, in which, behind the rise and fall of civilizations, certain transcendent purposes are being progressively, although not deliberately, fulfilled. Whereas Toynbee had previously regarded the universal church, in which the insight of a higher religion is institutionalized, as a chrysalis out of which a new civilization would eventually emerge, he now proposes a "reversal of roles" (VII, 420). It is a civilization, he now maintains, which is the more appropriately regarded as a chrysalis. For it is through the experiences of internal proletariats that the higher religions arise. It is through the suffering consequent upon the breakdown of civilization that man progresses in knowledge of God.

The elaboration of this new viewpoint enables Toynbee to reintroduce into his account of the total experiences of civilized man a linear rather than a merely cyclical pattern; and it suggests to him a purposive significance for the historical process as a whole. The goal of history, he now tells us—the whole point of the rise and fall of civilizations (which is like the monotonous turning of a wheel)—is to enable man to pass beyond the merely civilized state altogether (this being comparable to the forward movement of the vehicle to which the wheel is attached). Just as the rise of first generation civilizations constitutes a change of such tremendous importance that it deserves to be called a social "mutation," so Toynbee envisages, mutating out of a disintegrating civilization, a new religious species of society organized around a universal church. At times he appears to believe that the medieval Christian Church almost achieved such a terrestrial City of God. Its failure seems to have been due, in Toynbee's view, to the fatal error of the Papacy in taking up the sword.

Far, far back, at the beginning of his *Study*, when remarking on the vast numbers of primitive societies which had to come into being and pass away before civilized man appeared at all, Toynbee had contemplated with equanimity the prospect of a correspondingly long career for the civilized species of society. By the time he formulates his new conception of the significance of universal churches, however, he has become so impatient that he castigates all civilizations of the third generation, including his own, as "vain repetitions of the heathen" (VII, 445). For the four existing higher religions now embodied in universal churches all arose in the disintegration phases of two civilizations of the second generation: the Indic and the Syriac. And Toynbee, in what is progressively revealed as his post-Christian phase, not only regards these religions as of more or less equal value, but seems also unable any longer to envisage the possibility of further religious insight being achieved by the emergence of a new crop of higher religions out of the dissolution of the third generation civilizations now alive. Civilizations of the second generation were *necessary,* and hence not "vain repetitions," because, as far as Toynbee has been able to discover, the spiritual resources available in the internal proletariats of first generation civilizations were not sufficient to allow more than rudimentary higher religions to arise—none of them succeeding in establishing a universal church. Our need now, as Toynbee sees it, is not for further insight. It is for the social application of the insight civilized men already possess.

Toynbee's hope for the future appears to be that the four universal churches, the similarities of which he seems greatly to exaggerate, will in some unexplained way either work together or coalesce—producing (in a typically Toynbean image) heavenly music on earth, in four part harmony (VII, 428). With this project in view, he relents somewhat about the alleged meaninglessness of the career of Western Civilization. Some virtue may still be ascribed to it if, in progressing toward its own eventual disintegration, it unites the world in some soon to be established universal political community. For this may provide the seedbed for a synthesis of the higher religions in some new all-embracing universal church. In the course of his speculations as to the form its syncretistic faith might take, Toynbee composes a litany, of which the following is a sample:

> *Christe, audi nos.*
> Christ Tammuz, Christ Adonis, Christ Osiris, Christ Balder, hear us by whatsoever name we bless Thee for suffering death for our salvation.
> *Christe Jesu, exaudi nos.*
> Buddha Gautama, show us the path that will lead us out of our afflictions.
> *Sancta Dei Genetrix, intercede pro nobis.*
> Mother Mary, Mother Isis, Mother Cybele, Mother Ishtar, Mother Kwanyin, have compassion on us, by whatsoever name we bless thee for bringing Our Saviour into the World.
> *Sancte Michael, intercede pro nobis.*
> Mithras, fight at our side in our battle of Light against Darkness.
> *Omnes Sancti Angeli et Archangeli, intercedite pro nobis.*
> All ye devoted bodhisattvas, who for us your fellow living beings and for our release have forborne, aeon after aeon, to enter into your rest, tarry with us, we beseech you, yet a little while longer . . . [X, 143].

The empirical method   There is much more of the poet and seer in Toynbee than can even be hinted at in such a stark outline of his system. There is also much magnificent history. Our interest, however, is in the claim he makes to advance his conclusions on the basis of what he calls his "trusty and well-beloved method of making an empirical survey" (IV, 261). Of these, the most distinctive, of course, is his claim to have established a number of laws of history; and in suggesting lines of possible criticism, it is the latter we shall have chiefly in mind. To other aspects of what he says, some of the considerations already raised in connection with Hegel's theory, and to be raised later in connection with Niebuhr's, will also be found to apply.

It is commonly objected against Toynbee, both that the evidence he adduces for his generalizations is too slight, and that the direction his inquiry takes in amassing it is methodologically misguided. With, at most, some thirty-two specimens of the species "civilization" to work with—almost a third of which (the abortive and arrested civilizations) are conceded, in any case, not to have displayed a normal pattern of development—the complaint is that he simply does not have (and no one could possibly have) the data to assert his generalizations as "laws." This is especially, although not exclusively, true of what has been called Toynbee's "most significant generalization": [7] the assertion that civilizations develop in response to a challenge of adversity, grow through a series of responses to successive challenges, each arising out of the response to the last, break down through eventual failure to respond to a repeated challenge, and disintegrate into a dominant minority and an internal and external proletariat. Even with respect to the materials he has, it is often claimed, his inquiry does not really assume the form of an empirical "survey." For as Toynbee himself admits, his actual procedure was, first, to note a likeness between Hellenic and Western societies, achieving thereby a "binocular view of history," and to go on then to search for similar patterns in societies with which he was less familiar (X, 95; V, 58). This, it is argued, is no way to inquire empirically into the life cycles of civilizations—although it is a very good way to *impose* a pattern on the more remote examples. It is the method not of the empirical survey, but of the Procrustean Bed.

There is force in both of these objections. Yet Toynbee's critics often overstate it. [8] With respect to the first, for example, there is a feature of his practice which makes it quite misleading to represent him as generalizing, straight off, from a mere twenty to thirty-two cases. His generalizations may not represent a very high level of scientific theorizing about the world; but they are not simple inductions. They have a considerable additional tissue of support in the constant reference he makes to what, with the general knowledge of human nature he assumes we already possess, we may expect the protagonists to do and achieve in circumstances typical of the various stages of a civilization's career. An attempt is also made to do this for deviations from the standard pattern; these are not simply reported, but in every case something like an explanation of the deviation is offered. With respect to the second objection, it might be argued, too, that Toynbee's practice of beginning with an actual case, which is used as a standard of com-

[7] J. W. Blyth, "Toynbee and the Categories of Interpretation," *Philosophical Review*, LVIII (1949), 361.

[8] For further discussion of this and other criticisms of Toynbee's methodology, see M. Ashley Montagu, ed., *Toynbee and History: Critical Essays and Reviews* (Boston: Porter Sargent, Publisher, 1956).

parison for further ones, is simply a variation on the normal use of a hypothesis. The fact that the hypothesis was itself derived from knowledge of a prior actual case need not affect its status adversely. This is not to say that Toynbee's laws *have* sufficient empirical support (his explanations often appear to be of the wrong kind to provide it), or that he does not often in fact display a little *too* much dexterity in arranging what is known of the more remote civilizations into the Hellenic-Western pattern. The point is that neither consideration affords an objection to empirical philosophy of history, Toynbee-style, as such; and both *have* been so represented.

The actual empirical adequacy of Toynbee's account has in fact been weighed for over a generation, on a scale without precedent in speculation about history. The very nature of his theory, of course, leaves it open to objections on a very broad front; indeed, Toynbee is a fair target for every historical specialist into whose little corner of universal history he so much as takes a step. Where Hegel could legitimately ignore anything which did not contribute to the specific explanatory story he was telling, Toynbee is committed to showing that the career of *every* civilization (unless special circumstances can be shown) conforms to the laws he claims to have discovered. Even *his* encyclopedic knowledge, it is now generally agreed, proves unequal to the weight of generalization placed upon it. More seriously, the kind of criticism on points of detail that has often been urged against him suggests (as in the case of Hegel) that the disputed conclusions he draws often owe as much to their being required for his theory as to independent examination of the evidence. The charge of employing a "Procrustean Bed," in other words, may have substance after all. Of a very extensive literature which could be cited in illustration of this, two examples will suffice for our purposes. Both are derived from the writings of Pieter Geyl, already referred to, whose own response to the challenge of Toynbee's *Study* has earned him the title of the "Anti-Toynbee." [9]

The first relates to Toynbee's explanation of the triumph of the English colonists in North America over their French and Dutch rivals, which is cited as a small-scale exemplification of "challenge-and-response." According to Toynbee, what is significant is the fact that bleak New England provided the victors with an optimum environmental challenge by contrast with the much too difficult and much too easy ground facing settlers to the north and south of them. Nothing but the desire to find a confirming instance of his challenge-and-response formula, Geyl declares, could have led Toynbee to discuss this matter, as he does, without reference to external, and much more important, factors like the role of English seapower in the struggle. For the historical problem here is not a particularly obscure or difficult one; the error is not one that could be excused by reference to the un-

---

[9] *Debates with Historians*, chaps. V-VIII, especially pp. 105-8.

derstandable ignorance of a non-specialist. A similar and equally inexcusable blindness to the total situation under discussion is Geyl's explanation of a second strange contention, this time made by Toynbee in the course of illustrating his theory of the "withdrawal-and-return" of creative minorities. Great Britain, we are told, withdrew from Western society into creative isolation, roughly from the defeat of the Spanish Armada to the rise of modern Germany. "The Glorious Revolution [which occurred during this period] is indeed a fine example of the great deeds which England was to achieve through her seclusion!" Geyl explodes. "Have William the Third and his Dutchmen been forgotten?" Even after making allowances for Geyl's national pride—his opposition to Toynbee is not unrelated to his being one of the most nationalist of historians—it seems fair to accept his interpretation of these two examples. What they suggest is that long before Toynbee stands revealed, toward the end of his *Study*, as a religious prophet, with minimal interest in the course of history for its own sake, he had already shown signs of having, by his repeated neglect of context, lost the judgment of a historian. It is this, rather than a simple failure of historical knowledge, or even his asking unusually wide-ranging questions about history, that really lies behind his widespread indictment by members of the historical fraternity.

The conceptual apparatus
But the assessment of Toynbee's empirical claims is not simply a matter of checking the accuracy of historical details. Equally important is the question of the logical adequacy of the conceptual foundations of his system, and of the hypotheses which are to be tested. Toynbee's *Study*, after all, even if it aims at a good deal more than can be accomplished by scientific thinking, and in spite of its copious use of "literary" modes of persuasion, has at least in part the declared aim "to try out the scientific approach to human affairs and to test how far it will carry us." [10] It is a common charge against Toynbee, however, that his conceptual apparatus is so vague, so ill thought out, so question-begging, that it is often difficult to determine exactly what he is asserting, and on the basis of what argument he asserts it.

A simple, but crucial, example of such difficulty can be seen in his treatment of the concept of a "civilization"—the central concept of his *Study*. When this term is first introduced, it is given the meaning of "an intelligible field of enquiry." The implied contrast is with nations or city-states, which are not regarded as intelligible units because of the contacts with other political components of their own civilizations which make it impossible to treat them as relatively isolated causal systems. In the course of his analysis of disintegration, however, it becomes clear that Toynbee's civilizations themselves have exactly the same kind of contact with other societies, thus destroying the original

---

[10] "What I Am Trying to Do," reprinted in *Toynbee and History*, ed. Montagu, p. 6.

basis of contrast. The original definition had in any case been tacitly abandoned; for the course of Toynbee's argument had shown civilizations in significant contact with each other even during the growth stage. By the time this becomes apparent, however, Toynbee's interest has switched from civilizations to churches. The concept is never clarified.

A further illustration of the vagueness of the same concept is to be found in the criterion by which Toynbee distinguishes civilizations from primitive societies. The latter, he says, are static; but he goes on to admit that they must at one time have been dynamic. In their own way, they thus display an ossified response to an ancient challenge. But how, if this is true, are we to distinguish primitive societies from arrested civilizations? Toynbee does not say. It is essential, however, that he should do so, for otherwise he is open to the charge that his laws of civilizations apply only to a group of cases selected from the whole class of societies on no specifiable principle. And this would rob them of determinate empirical force.

In an author who claims to be showing his benighted fellow historians how far scientific method can take them, such lapses are far from trivial. It would not require many of them, at any rate, to vitiate any *predictions* derived from his theory; and Toynbee does often give the impression that prediction is one of his aims. If this appears to overstate the case, an example of conceptual difficulty closer to the main course of Toynbee's argument may be cited. Let us look at what he says in explanation of the breakdown of a civilization. The breakdown, he tells us at one point, is *caused* by a failure of creativity in the minority. But he tells us too that the failure of creativity in this same minority is the *criterion* of breakdown in a civilization (V, 17). And he clearly cannot say both of these things without emptying his thesis of all significance. If creative failure is a criterion, then indeed the universal "law" has been established that whenever we find such a failure, we find a society that has broken down. But this, of course, now becomes a mere logical truism—a tautology—with no empirical force. If it is Toynbee's thesis, on the other hand, that breakdown is *caused* by a failure of the minority, then the empirical force of the alleged "law" will be restored. But we shall then be thoroughly in the dark as to what exactly it is that is said to be the result of this cause. And we shall remain so until Toynbee enunciates another, and logically independent, criterion of breakdown. Once again, it should perhaps be emphasized that difficulties of this kind do not warrant criticism of the whole "idea" of Toynbee's inquiry; they are matters, chiefly, of faulty execution. The logical "repair work" they make necessary, however, appears to be extensive; and it would require a sympathetic, liberal interpretation of Toynbee's presumed intent to carry it out.[11]

[11] For some suggestions as to how Toynbee might avoid the difficulties noted here and below, see my "Toynbee's Search for Historical Laws," *History and Theory*, I, No. 1 (1960), 32-54.

A conflict of   An even more commonly noted example of Toynbee's involvement
presuppositions   in logical difficulties centers around the account he gives of the
way the challenge-and-response formula is to be applied, especially
his comparisons in three terms. A challenge, Toynbee contends, must
be severe if it is to elicit a response, but not so severe that no response
is forthcoming at all. A *maximum* response is elicited, not by a maximum challenge, but by an *optimum* one. But since no criterion of
"optimum" challenge is presented, apart from its being one which elicits
a maximum response, *this* general "law" is also in danger of degenerat-
ing into a tautology. More embarrassing still, it is far from clear that,
even if Toynbee *had* an adequate independent criterion for calling a
challenge "optimum," it is open to him to assert, on empirical grounds,
the generalization "An optimum challenge elicits a maximum response."
For at numerous points he denies that he is a determinist with respect
to human actions. In discussing "encounters" between human beings,
he says, for example: "I believe that the outcome of such an encounter
would not be predictable, even if we had complete knowledge of all
the antecedent facts." And in a debate with Geyl he declared: "I am a
believer in free will; in man's freedom to respond with all his heart
and soul and mind when life presents him with a challenge." [12] It seems
clear that, as he understands it himself, Toynbee's indeterminism entails
the denial of any *law* of response to challenges of a specifiable kind.

Toynbee's indeterminism in fact raises a general problem for the
interpretation of his inquiry—and one which goes far beyond mere
questions of careless statement or conceptual ineptitude. For it is surely
arguable that any attempt to show *on libertarian principles* how far
scientific method will take us is bound to be either an elaborate sham
or a tissue of confusions. Certainly the methodological discussion which
Toynbee appends to one of the later volumes gives evidence of two
sets of basic postulates in an unhappy state of conflict. And his attempt
to reconcile them, in the nearest thing to an overtly metaphysical discussion in the whole of his work, is gropingly unsuccessful.

At the theoretical level, Toynbee's uneasiness about this shows
itself especially in a remarkable unclarity about the concept of "law"
itself. His proneness to slip into tautological assertion has already been
remarked. But even when his generalizations remain empirical, they
often deviate in another way from the notion of a universal statement
connecting classes of events: they are asserted as if they were merely
summary statements of past fact, without definite commitment to what
will happen in similar cases in the future. Thus in discussing the system
of the Osmanlis, Toynbee observes, "the lives of such Nomad empires
on cultivated ground had . . . usually been short"; in warning of the
dangers of nationalism, he declares, "the fratricidal war of ever-increas-
ing violence between parochial sovereign states had been by far the

[12] *Ibid.*; and Pieter Geyl, Arnold J. Toynbee, and Pitirim A. Sorokin, *The Pattern
of the Past: Can We Determine It?* (Boston: Beacon Press, Inc., 1949), p. 76.

commonest cause of mortality among civilizations"; and in examining the essential institutions of universal states, he argues for "a general rule that the written word had been an indispensable instrument of oecumenical government" (VII, 542; IX, 442; VII, 239). Toynbee has a fondness, too, for asserting his generalizations as if they stated only what happens "as a rule." Indeed, he refers at times—almost triumphantly—to exceptions as "proving the rule" (V, 3n; VII, 271; VIII, 542). There is a general reluctance in his work to give the impression that what he calls a "law" cannot be "broken."

Toynbee's conceptual and metaphysical uneasiness about "laws" is also reflected in his discussion of concrete issues. It is particularly evident in what he says in answer to the question which lay behind his undertaking the *Study* in the first place: that of the prospects of Western Civilization. Toynbee's examination of the last four hundred years of Western history in fact uncovers all the signs of breakdown which he discusses with such assurance when analyzing the courses run by alien civilizations, now dead (VI, 312ff; IX, 406ff). On the basis of these signs (although he is not entirely consistent about this) the breakdown of Western Civilization can be dated as long ago as the outbreak of the Wars of Religion of the sixteenth century. The ensuing Time of Troubles, after a minor rally in the comparatively peaceful and tolerant seventeenth and eighteenth centuries (when warfare, Toynbee says, was essentially the sport of kings) has been resumed in our own time in an orgy of nationalist struggles. By all arguments from analogy, we have experienced already one and a half beats of a fateful three and a half beat rhythm, and we are ripe for our universal state, a condition we narrowly missed in World War II. Nor are other indications of breakdown and disintegration difficult to find. Our dominant minority, for example, has been wrestling continuously with the recurring challenge of peace, with nothing better to offer than the monotonously unsuccessful response of defense. The tremendous geographical expansion of the West at the expense of primitive societies and alien civilizations alike, itself an ominous sign, has recruited an internal proletariat of antagonistic national minorities, descendants of African slaves, economically exploited workers, rootless intelligentsia, which rivals that of the Roman Empire. It is true that traces of an *external* proletariat are much more difficult to find, in consequence of the virtual obliteration of the last barbarian frontiers. But, asks Toynbee, with characteristic resourcefulness, do we not find a much more terrible barbarism breaking out right in our midst, in the adventures of the National Socialists and their kind?

In view of such considerations—which are reinforced by the discovery of certain attitudes in the West which are typical of an age of disintegration—it would appear that the judgment required by Toynbee's own comparative study is that Western Civilization is as good as doomed, and that our future prospects permit only various kinds of delaying action. This conclusion, however, is one Toynbee repeatedly refuses to draw—even in the final volumes, in which, as many critics have remarked, the survival of the West appears to become a matter of less and less importance to him as his hopes for a religious "mutation" rise. The analysis of the first six volumes actually closes with the hope that God will grant us a "reprieve"—which we shall doubtless receive, Toynbee assures us, provided we ask for it "in a contrite spirit and with a broken heart" (VI, 320). Yet the only basis for such a hope that appears in the whole of his *Study* is Toynbee's libertarian metaphysical beliefs. For he claims to have shown, at cost of tremendous labor, that there are *no precedents whatever* for a revival of creativity in a civilization that has once broken down.

A RELIGIOUS APPROACH

8

Reinhold Niebuhr   With Niebuhr we leave metaphysical speculation and quasi-scientific proofs for an attempt to "interpret" history from the standpoint of religious faith. It is Niebuhr's contention that nothing less than divine revelation, as elaborated in Christian theology, affords an "adequate" basis for discerning the meaning of historical events. Whether his own "neo-orthodox" Protestantism can properly be regarded as yielding *the* Christian view of history is, of course, a further question—and a controversial one. Niebuhr's fellow Christians have often attacked him, either for finding too little, or for finding too much, religious significance in events. And a considerable part of his own energies have been directed toward combating what he regards as dangerous Christian heresies about history. Such intramural theological disputes, however, must be regarded as lying beyond our scope. It should be understood that in referring hereafter to Niebuhr's views as "Christian" there is no thought of trying to decide them.

For Niebuhr himself, the working out of a Christian view of history is closely associated with the task of showing the relevance of religious faith to the problems of secular life—especially political ones; and he is probably as well known in America for his dour and radical comment on political affairs as for his theological scholarship. The most authoritative statement of his theological position is given in his two-volume Gifford Lectures, *The Nature and Destiny of Man.*[1] The doctrines which are of special importance for the interpretation of history, however, have been given shorter and more popular expression in a volume entitled *Faith and History;*[2] and it is largely from this that the

[1] (New York: Charles Scribner's Sons, 1941-43). *The Philosophy of History in Our Time*, ed. Meyerhoff, contains an excerpt from this, pp. 313-45.

[2] (New York: Charles Scribner's Sons, 1949). Page references in the text are to this work.

exposition of his theory in this chapter will be drawn. Even the popular work, it must be admitted, is often heavy going for the uninitiated. Its language is elusively theological; its argument irritatingly loose and repetitious. And it appears at times to indulge in paradoxical and mysterious utterance for its own sake. Yet, in its own prophetic way, Niebuhr's work makes a considerable impact. And it has the advantage, for our purposes, of having been widely discussed.

Three views   Like Hegel, Niebuhr introduces his own interpretation by contrast-
of history   ing it with two rival views which he regards as erroneous. The first
of these he calls the Greek classical. Niebuhr does not claim that the Greeks were entirely agreed in their approach to history. Heraclitus, for example, stands outside the tradition he has in mind, and so does Dionysian religion. But with reference especially to Plato, Aristotle, and the Stoics, he thinks it justifiable to speak of a common classical approach.

This approach finds the intelligibility of history in its "subjection to natural recurrence" rather than in "the novelties which human freedom introduces into the temporal process" (p. 64). Meaning is attributed only to the extent to which the historical process reflects or exemplifies certain timeless, rational forms. Such a view, Niebuhr observes, diverts attention from everything *we* should regard as distinctively historical; and it discourages men from dealing creatively with the unique situations in which they find themselves. It represents, in fact, a "western intellectual version of a universal type of ahistorical spirituality" found in nonintellectual, mystical forms in various Oriental religions (p. 16). Like them, it looks for escape from the perplexities and particularity of historical existence into a world—in this case a world of pure thought—which transcends history altogether. Viewed in this way, history is, at best, derivatively meaningful; it is not meaningful "in its wholeness" (p. 64).

At the opposite end of the scale is the modern Western view. This finds historical significance *entirely* in the unique effects of human freedom and in the linear, developmental pattern of events which results. A post-Renaissance phenomenon, arising at a time when Western man experienced a surge of confidence in his creative powers, this view of history actually traces its ancestry back to the insights of the Hebrew prophets, although in secularizing them, Niebuhr goes on to argue, it misunderstands them. The essence of the modern view is that history, which classical man regarded as cycles of natural growth and decay, is seen as "a realm of indeterminate growth"; and by this is meant "growth of mind or of sympathy, of the inclusive purposes which increasing reason supposedly guarantees" (p. 68). These purposes are variously interpreted as increasing control over nature, increasing physical well-being, the democratization of society, universal community, or other desirable states of affairs. The fundamental belief, however, is that "growth means freedom; and freedom, as in classical thought, is assumed to be rational freedom." In this respect, a philosopher of history like Hegel only puts more subtly what most Western theorists of history have believed.

From the Christian standpoint, Niebuhr concedes, this modern view is an improvement on the classical because it finds meaning in the details of man's actual historical existence. But it involves its holder in a disastrous naïveté. For in envisaging increasing human freedom as guaranteeing a rational social progress it seriously overestimates both the *extent* to which freedom increases in history and the *connection* between freedom and virtue. This issues in the false conclusion that it may be possible eventually to change the whole "human situation" (pp. 15-16)—a possibility expressing itself in utopian projections of various kinds. In fact, the most casual glance at the course of history will show that the growth of human freedom and power simply "enlarges the scope of human problems" (p. 98). Perhaps no definite limit can be set to the potential extent of human powers over nature; and history has certainly been the scene of great technical advances. But the power that matters in history is man's mastery over his own "egoistic desires and impulses." And each apparent advance gives the latter "a wider range than they had under more primitive conditions." Thus,

> Modern industrial society dissolved ancient forms of political authoritarianism; but the tyrannies which grew on its soil proved more brutal and vexatious than the old ones. The inequalities rooted in landed property were levelled. But the more dynamic inequalities of a technical society became more perilous to the community than the more static forms of uneven power. The achievement of individual liberty was one of the genuine advances of bourgeois society. But this society also created atomic individuals, who, freed of the disciplines of the older organic communities, were lost in the mass; and became the prey of demagogues and charlatans who transmuted their individual anxieties and resentments into collective political power of demonic fury [p. 7].

The Christian view, according to Niebuhr, is protected against the naïve expectations of the progress theory by its more realistic account of human nature: On this view, the evil we find in history is not regarded as an accidental or transient thing; it is located in the permanent human condition of "original sin," symbolized by the "Fall." In simplest terms, what this doctrine asserts is "the obvious fact that all men are persistently inclined to regard themselves more highly and are more assiduously concerned with their own interests than any 'objective' view of their importance would warrant." [3] In more technical theological language, sin is the tendency of man to rebel against God—or, what is the same thing, against the limits of his creaturely status—so that he makes of himself a "false center of meaning." It is the Christian claim that sin, so conceived, is an exercise of human freedom; "it is not by

[3] *The Irony of American History* (New York: Charles Scribner's Sons, 1952), p. 15.

nature but in freedom that men sin" (p. 122). Thus there is little to be expected from the mere increase of freedom and power. This is a doctrine, Niebuhr adds, which is not confined in its application to individuals; for nations and institutions also have recognizable "wills" and "interests" (p. 91). The inclination to deny his own "finiteness" is, in fact, "particularly evident in the collective life of mankind" (p. 114).

The Christian view of man collides head on with what Niebuhr takes to be the underlying assumption of most progress theories: that historical evil is a result mainly of man's incomplete emancipation from nature; that human self-interest and pride are due to a "culture lag" (p. 11), which will be overcome as man progressively exchanges the role of "creature" for that of "creator" of history. On the modern view, "history redeems man from nature" (p. 68); for the Christian, history is not "redemptive." There are cultural continuities and patterns which give a kind of meaning, or at any rate interest, to the course of events. Niebuhr does not deny these; indeed, he criticizes Toynbee, not for finding patterns, but for underestimating their extent and complexity. He concedes to Hegel, too, that history is, among other things, the story of "the development of freedom." What he denies is the moral superiority of men living in Hegel's rational state. If history is to be meaningful, for Niebuhr, it must make moral sense. From the standpoint of this concern, it is under constant "threat of meaninglessness" (p. 121) because of the destructive use to which man puts his freedom.

God's sovereignty over history So much for what, according to Niebuhr, the Christian view denies. What does it *assert* about history? The simplest answer is that it asserts the sovereignty of God over the whole of it. "All historical destinies," declares Niebuhr, "are under the dominion of a single divine sovereignty," which thus provides a "general frame of meaning" for historical events (pp. 107, 20). It is because of this, not because of any unity which can be rationally demonstrated, or which can be ascertained by an empirical survey, that "history is potentially and ultimately one story" (p. 112).

This is an idea, Niebuhr says, which comes to us from the ancient Hebrews. Like most of their neighbors, they had a belief in a "more potent power than any human will" which was at work in their national history. But they gave this idea a distinctive form by conceiving the divine power neither as "the projection of the nation's or individual's ideals and purposes, nor as a power co-extensive with, or supplementary to, the nation's power" (p. 102). The relationship between God and Israel was expressed in the Sinaitic Covenant. But Israel did not choose God; God chose Israel, for His own mysterious purposes. The idea of the Covenant was interpreted and reinterpreted by the Hebrew prophets in the light of their historical experiences. These forced them to realize that a "chosen" people has no special immunity from disaster. If anything, special status seemed to carry with it special disabilities. The discovery that the divine sovereignty was not at the *disposal* of a particular people, and that God's purposes might be served even through the agency of Israel's enemies, and even at Israel's expense, led naturally to the idea of universal history as the matrix of those purposes. The Christian notion of the Second Covenant, not between God and any particular people, but rather between God and all believers—potentially all men—further develops the same idea.

So conceived, Niebuhr claims, divine sovereignty is "the basis of the first genuine conception of a universal history"; and it affords "the basis for the only possible universalism which does not negate or unduly simplify the meaning of history in the process of universalizing it" (p. 103). If God's sovereignty alone gives unity to history, however, in what way does it show itself, in the face of human rebellion against His purposes? According to Niebuhr, it does it in two chief ways. On the one hand, God places an "ultimate limit" upon human defiance; on the other, He affords opportunities for "rebirth and renewal" when men and nations repent (pp. 27-28, 124-25). The divine sovereignty is shown in its first aspect in the inevitable failures of men to make good their pretensions to be "centers of meaning" in history, this failure being interpreted by the Christian as a divine *judgment* upon the pretensions involved. It is shown in its second aspect of divine *grace* whenever men renounce their false pretensions; for grace "both searches out the evil character of sin and overcomes it" (p. 22). In view of this twofold activity of divine sovereignty within it, Niebuhr adds, history can be seen to have a dramatic theme of staggering proportions. It is nothing less than the story of "God's contest with all men" (p. 27); it displays His continuing struggle to overcome the corruptions of human freedom.

The account Niebuhr goes on to elaborate of the actual operation of divine providence in history is (like Toynbee's theory) in some ways reminiscent of the Hegelian dialectic. For Niebuhr's providence does not intervene miraculously; like Hegel's "reason" it is immanent in the historical process itself. It is part of the providential "structure of existence" that "forms of life which make themselves into their own end" accomplish thereby their own "ultimate self-destruction" (p. 27). By a kind of divine nemesis, pride not only goes before a fall; it brings it about. There is thus a vaguely cyclic pattern in history after all: men and nations are constantly overreaching themselves and being brought low. Unlike the Hegelian dialectic, however, Niebuhr's tension between providence and a corrupt human freedom has no dynamic quality; there is no progress from synthesis to synthesis. The limiting power of providence explains not the direction history takes, but why history never gets anywhere at all.

The providential dialectic of history has a further interesting feature: it is *ironical*. Irony arises out of an incongruous contrast of some kind: a contrast, say, between a nation's pretensions and its actual achievements. To be ironical, however, the contrast must not be merely fortuitous; one element must be the hidden source of the other. Thus a powerful man or nation, revealed in reality to be weak, is involved in irony only if the weakness is due to some pretense of strength. A wise man who behaves foolishly is involved in irony only if his foolishness is derived from some pretension of wisdom. Niebuhr finds such irony in the fact that the crucifixion of Christ was accomplished by the representatives of the best legal system and the purest religion of the day; being "perfect," neither could countenance any appeal to higher authority. He finds it equally in such secular historical circumstances as the present defense postures of East and West. It is the very success of defense research in furnishing "efficient" nuclear weapons that has made both sides feel so insecure. American history, Niebuhr claims, is especially open to ironic interpretation. There is irony, for example, in the fact that it was those who wished to protect their own excessive economic power who most enthusiastically seized on the Jeffersonian critique of strong central government, originally propounded in the interests of the weak; and in the fact that, with the passage of time, it has been that very concentration of political power at the center which has alone proved capable of protecting the weak. According to Niebuhr, Christianity

> tends to make the ironic view of human evil in history the normative one. Its conception of redemption from evil carries it beyond the limits of irony, but its interpretation of the nature of evil in human history is consistently ironic. This consistency is achieved on the basis of the belief that the whole drama of human history is under the scrutiny of a divine judge who laughs at human pretensions without being hostile to human aspirations. The laughter at the pretensions is the divine judgment. The judgment is transmuted into mercy if it results in abating the pretensions and in prompting men to a contrite recognition of the vanity of their imagination.[4]

Meaning and obscurity

When all this has been said, however, Niebuhr is forced to allow that the evidences of divine sovereignty actually observable in the course of history are obscure and inexact. "Moral judgments are executed in history," he insists, "but never with precision" (p. 129); indeed, "human defiance and evil seem to enjoy long periods of immunity" (p. 125). Similarly, although there are "new beginnings" in history, by divine grace, the historical process as a whole is "not progressively emancipated from evil" (p. 136). History cannot therefore be said, on the Christian view, to be completely meaningful. It is (in Niebuhr's curious terminology) only "potentially" or "provisionally" meaningful; there are only "tangents" or "facets" of meaning in it (pp. 114, 125, 132, 233).

The reason for this residual moral obscurity lies in the fact, already noted, that providence does not operate through miraculous interventions; it uses historical instruments, and these are always morally defective. Advancing social forces, which are "from the absolute standpoint, instruments of divine justice upon all established institutions, are

[4] *The Irony of American History*, p. 133.

always involved in the same idolatries against which they contend" (pp. 227-28). They are "not content to be instruments of providence," but set themselves up, in turn, as false centers of historical significance— a truth sadly illustrated, according to Niebuhr, by the proletarian revolutions of our time. Both judgment and grace, as they operate in history, are necessarily related to the "morally irrelevant factor of power" (p. 129). Unscrupulous nations are punished only "if sufficient power is aligned to implement the moral condemnation which the victims of their tyranny sense inwardly." Nor is social virtue necessarily rewarded. From the standpoint of historical survival, it is possible to be *too* pure— for example, by adopting an unrealistically defenseless position. Christian love, Niebuhr observes wryly, if not indeed a bit cynically, "is normative for, but not tenable in, history" (p. 143). It is significant, he adds, that Christ himself suffered historical defeat. Even when a moral use of power occurs, the moral meaning of history may be obscured by the fact that all destruction of social evil involves suffering by the innocent. The operation of divine grace is similarly defective. Renewals never succeed entirely in overcoming the "contradictions of man's historic existence." An especially bitter example of this all-pervasiveness of "original sin" is the failure of the Christian missionaries of the West to free themselves of the imperialistic taint of their cultural background. According to Niebuhr, indeed, some of the worst evils in history have entered it as "schemes of redemption" (p. 214)—including Christian ones.

Confronted, as they were, with the partly "hidden" character of divine sovereignty, and sensing "a divine judgment above and beyond the rough and inexact historical judgments," the Hebrew prophets naturally looked for "more perfect and exact divine retribution in a future messianic age" (p. 126). This was envisaged as a reign of justice in which all the moral obscurities of history would be finally resolved. In the expectancy which this view establishes towards the future, Niebuhr regards it as the genesis of the progress theory. But it differs drastically from the latter in regarding the moral resolution of history as occurring through an intervention of some kind from without, which would involve a change in the whole condition of man. There is no assumption that history itself would gradually achieve messianic conditions. The qualitative difference between the present and the messianic ages—analogous, it might be noted, to that which divides the present age of class struggle, in Marxist theory, from the final classless society— is symbolized in Old Testament thought by such notions as the lion lying down with the lamb.

The New Testament figure of the Antichrist, who comes at the end of history, is an explicit repudiation, not only of progressive utopianism, but also of the messianic hope. The Antichrist symbolizes the Christian belief that history as a whole, in spite of piecemeal judgments and renewals, will remain "morally ambiguous" to the end (p. 135); there is no question of the total enterprise being emancipated from evil, either progressively or miraculously. The "most explicit forms of evil," in fact, are envisaged as coming late in history (p. 136). There is even, Niebuhr points out, the "awesome suggestion" that the faith itself might vanish from the earth (p. 112). Even this, however, would not mean "the defeat of God." For the Christian view also envisages a Last Judgment and General Resurrection. The symbol of the Last Judgment expresses the Christian confidence that there *is* a judgment beyond the inexact ones of ordinary history, while at the same time renouncing the belief that it will be made *within* history. The symbol of the Resurrection implies that God has resources of love and mercy for the *final* overcoming of evil, although once again this is beyond the possibilities of history itself. The symbols of Christian eschatology point to a transhistorical reality which can be "sensed" or "apprehended by faith." For the Christian, Niebuhr declares, "the grace of God completes the structure of meaning beyond the limits of rational intelligibility in the realm of history" (p. 103).

Of all the claims made by Niebuhr for the Christian view of history, perhaps three might be singled out for critical comment here. The first is the contention that the Biblical view of man's nature and situation is more realistic than alternatives; the second, that the Christian view of the meaning of the course of events can, to some extent at least, be verified or validated; the third, that "mystery" as well as "meaning" must be incorporated in an adequate interpretation of history—the recognition of this being a special merit, not a defect, of the Christian view.

Freedom and original sin
According to Niebuhr, only the Christian view of history "deals with the problems of evil ultimately" (p. 22). The doctrine of original sin counteracts any facile assumption of the possibility of human perfectibility through "self-development." At the same time, the doctrine of divine grace assures us that, although "enmeshed in a historical fate," man is never completely beyond redemption. Niebuhr's whole theory of the historical tension between a sinful human freedom on the one hand, and divine providence on the other, however, clearly invites analysis of the elusive theological concepts employed. Something has already been said about the allegedly immanent character of judgment and grace. What shall we say of the notion of original sin itself and its relation to human freedom?

Original sin, it will be remembered, was defined as the inclination of all men to rebel against God and to make themselves false centers of meaning. Put shortly, and less theologically, it is an inclination to self-centeredness and to self-interested action—an inclination which perhaps most of Niebuhr's critics would grant to have some basis in fact. A difficulty arises, however, over the denial that this inclination is a "natural" disposition ("it is not by nature but in freedom that men sin"). For in spite of this, the doctrine of original sin is regarded by Niebuhr as an adequate basis for doing what Hegel expressly avoided, and even Toynbee hesitated about: predicting the future course of history. Niebuhr's prediction, it is true, is not very specific. It is limited to the claim—in opposition to the modern view—that no significant moral progress will take place. Yet it is a prediction all the same. The question arises whether this does not introduce an incoherence into Niebuhr's theory like that into which Toynbee's was suspected to fall.

There is no question that Niebuhr *does* assert the reality of human freedom. According to him, history is "the fruit and proof of man's freedom." And freedom is conceived as introducing genuine novelty into history; this is what distinguishes it from nature. What then did Niebuhr mean by freedom? H. D. Lewis has argued that his use of the concept is thoroughly confused: that he slides between several quite different senses of the term.[5] Sometimes he seems chiefly to mean rationality or coherence in action—thus approximating to the notion of "free action" often employed by idealist metaphysicians. At other times he seems rather to mean self-determination—by contrast with the determination of action by something "external" to the agent. Occasionally, no more seems to be meant than *awareness* of the necessities under which actions are performed, this being interpreted as a way of "transcending" them. Niebuhr's most usual sense, however, is the more familiar one of a degree of "emancipation from natural necessity": a possibility of acting in a way not predictable through knowledge of any laws of nature, including human nature (pp. 93, 124). It is true that Niebuhr emphasizes strongly certain limitations upon such "emancipation." Thus he reminds us that even in historically significant action, man remains a part of the physical and biological world. He is a creature of a certain sex, for example; and even the saints, although they tried, were unable entirely to transcend their sexuality, as the unconscious erotic symbolism of their utterance often shows. We are reminded, too, that all action is performed in a historical context which, to the agent himself, is to a large extent *given*. Thus no one can undo the tremendous changes that have taken place in Europe as a result of Hitler's adventures, or start from scratch in race relations in an America which earlier trafficked in Negro slaves. Such considerations, however, only count against a doctrine which no sensible libertarian has ever held: that man's choice of action is unlimited. They warrant the conclusion only that there are certain things which men *cannot* do; not that there are certain things which it can be predicted they *will* do.

It may appear that we could interpret Niebuhr's doctrine of original sin in similar fashion as simply placing a limit upon the choices open to human beings. In a troublesome, but crucial, passage, he declares: "The self finds itself free; but, as Augustine suggested, not free to do good." We might take this to mean that man's inclination to self-centeredness is also something "given"—something which limits human freedom without making actions predictable. It is doubtful,

[5] *Freedom and History* (London: George Allen & Unwin, 1962), pp. 221ff.

however, that Niebuhr's own view is as cogent as this. For the whole passage from which the quotation from Augustine is drawn goes like this:

> The real self . . . is involved in the evils, particularly the evils of self-seeking, which it commits. The self is always sufficiently emancipated of natural necessity, not to be compelled to follow the course dictated by self-interest. If it does so nevertheless, it is held culpable both in the court of public opinion and in the secret of its own heart. . . . The self seeks its own despite its freedom to envisage a wider good than its own interest [pp. 93-94].

Under pressure to make his theory morally acceptable—to rationalize the agreement of his religious position with the common-sense view that self-interestedness is "culpable"—Niebuhr concedes that the choices open to men *do* include the seeking of a "wider good." Yet at many other points he appears to deny this possibility. Original sin is said to be "a corruption which has a *universal* domination over all men"; man's defiance of God is "a *permanent* factor in history"; the Fall "symbolizes an *inevitable* . . . corruption of human freedom" (pp. 122, 140, 33. My italics). To add, in the latter instance, that the corruption, although inevitable, is "not natural" (Niebuhr calls this the "mystery" of original sin) looks very much like playing with words. For the corruption is, at any rate, something Niebuhr is willing to bet on.

Revelation and validation   The difficulty is focused by the term "inclination." Niebuhr's use of it often appears to be a calculated attempt to prevent the Christian view from falling unequivocally into either determinism or libertarianism, proper. It seems to be essential for his view of history as morally significant but not morally cumulative that he somehow have it both ways. The difficulty here will be regarded by many critics as no isolated one: they will see it as a frustrating, but quite characteristic, feature of theological thinking generally. And we do, in fact, find something of a similar kind if we go on to ask our second question: on what grounds the Christian view is recommended by Niebuhr to his readers.

Now it may seem that what Niebuhr has to say about history would not be offered as "verifiable" in any empirical sense. The Christian view sets out to interpret what happens in the light of the dogmas of Christian theology. But the latter are given through revelation, not through reason or experience. It is partly with this in mind that Niebuhr insists that he does not offer a philosophy of history at which one might arrive "by analyzing the sequences and recurrences, the structures and patterns of history" (pp. 26-27). Christianity, he says, "knows by faith of some events in history in which the transcendent source and end of the whole panorama of history is disclosed" (p. 22). Such an event is "the life, death and resurrection of Christ"—the last in a series of "God's mighty acts." Not that the latter are always recognized as such. For they "must be apprehended by faith, and can only be so apprehended in humility and repentance" (pp. 26-27). Reception of the divine revelation is itself a "gift of grace."

Yet Niebuhr, like Hegel, will not renounce entirely the claim to find something like empirical verification of his interpretation of history. It is not possible, he declares, to present a "rationally compelling" argument for the Christian view. But it is possible to give a "limited rational validation" of it: to "prove its relevance rationally" (p. 101). This is done, he says, in two ways.

> Negatively, the Gospel must and can be validated by exploring the limits of historic forms of wisdom and virtue. Positively, it is validated when the truth of faith is correlated with all truths which may be known by scientific and philosophical disciplines and proves itself a resource for coordinating them into a deeper and wider system of coherence [p. 152].

The negative way was sketched in Niebuhr's preliminary comparison of the Christian with the other two views of history, the latter being shown to provide "an inadequate view of the total human situation" (p. 164). The positive way involves interpreting specific happenings as manifestations of human sin and repentance, and of divine judgment and grace. According to Niebuhr, "all the known facts of history verify the interpretation of human destiny implied in New Testament eschatology."[6] On the other hand, the modern view especially is "in glaring contradiction" to "the facts of contemporary experience" (p. 30).

Niebuhr does, it is true, offer specific examples of the way he conceives the Christian view to fit the facts. His manner of doing so, however, raises difficulties for any easy acceptance of his claims. If his examples are to count as a genuine "validation," we need to know, not only that there are some events in history which, by exemplifying Niebuhr's theological concepts, give support to his interpretation as a whole, but also what, if it occurred, would count as evidence against that interpretation. And we need to know, too, that the signs of providence which are allegedly found in specific instances are recognized by virtue of clearly formulable criteria which are consistent with Niebuhr's position as a whole. On neither count is his "validation" very convincing.

As to the first difficulty: a critic's suspicions may well be aroused on finding Niebuhr declaring flatly that, for a Christian, "nothing can happen in history to shake the confidence in the meaning of existence" (p. 136). It might perhaps be thought that this is nothing more than an expression of conventional piety on Niebuhr's part. Yet his treatment of historical evidence often suggests that it is a good deal more than this. We find him arguing, for example, of the rise and fall of cultures and civilizations:

[6] *The Nature and Destiny of Man*, II, 319. Reprinted in *The Philosophy of History in Our Time*, ed. Meyerhoff, p. 329.

Their life is a testimony of the creativity of history, even as their death is a proof of the sin in history. The vast variety of historic organisms, the richness of their elaborations of human potentialities, the wealth of their many cultural forms and social configurations are as certainly a testimony to the divine providence under which they have grown, as their destruction is a vindication of the eternal judgment, which they are unable to defy with impunity.[7]

If a historic institution flowers, in other words, it is evidence of God's grace. If it withers, it is evidence of a divine judgment upon it. This form of argument, however, makes it virtually impossible to challenge Niebuhr's providential claims; his theory appears to have defenses against its own overthrow built right into it. Such a theory may still, of course, tell us the truth about history. But it is hard to see how it can claim to be *validated* by the facts of history to which it appeals.

Confidence in Niebuhr's "validations" will not be increased by examination of some of the more detailed applications of his principle of interpretation to historical circumstances. A good example is his contention that the rise of constitutional monarchy in Western Europe constitutes a "renewal" in history which must be attributed, in part, to divine grace.

Absolute monarchy has been destroyed in every nation in which modern conditions prevail. But the institution of constitutional monarchy has proved to be a most efficacious instrument of democracy in many of the most healthy of modern nations. Its virtue lies in its capacity to symbolize the permanent will of the national community in distinction to the momentary and shifting acts of will which are expressed and incarnated in particular governments. The political wisdom incorporated in constitutional monarchy is literally a wisdom vouchsafed to man "by grace." For neither the traditional proponents of monarchism nor its opponents had the wisdom to conceive the institution of constitutional monarchy. The former wanted to preserve its power unchanged and the latter wanted to destroy the institution. The emergence of this old institution in a new form did require that its defenders yield, however reluctantly, to new social forces in society. The monarch was shorn of his power; whereupon it was discovered that his powerlessness provided the community with a new form of power, which was completely compatible with the requirements of a more democratic justice [pp. 226-27].

But this is surely a most fanciful exemplification of "grace" in any other sense than that of "unmerited good fortune." With its heavy reliance on the mechanism of *prudence*, furthermore, it surely bears little relation to Niebuhr's general theory that "renewals" are (roughly at least) the rewards of repentance.

---

[7] *Ibid.*, p. 317. For further discussion of the problem of the verification of religious claims, see John Hick, *Philosophy of Religion*, Prentice-Hall Foundations of Philosophy Series, especially chap. 7.

The problem of validating Niebuhr's theory is not, of course, a single problem. His claim that there is no morally significant direction in history is comparatively straightforward; and it is to be tested, presumably, by reference to ordinary historical knowledge, and to the moral judgments we are prepared to make about past actions. To a considerable extent, this could be said also of Niebuhr's assertion of the ubiquity of original sin, understood as self-centeredness, if the difficulties about the formulation of the doctrine were met. When we move to the claim that there are evidences of divine judgment and grace in history, the question of validation becomes more difficult. But if the meaning of this claim is, at least in part, that people and institutions get their just deserts when their pride becomes overweening, and find fresh opportunities when they give up their false pretensions, then this too could certainly be submitted to the test of historical knowledge. And such testing, if not "proof" of the full theological meaning which Niebuhr would attribute to such patternings of events, might at any rate claim to show that history is "open" to a Christian interpretation.

As Niebuhr states it, however, there is an important part of the Christian view which appears to lie beyond the scope even of this limited sort of validation. For it is central to the Christian claim, we are told, that besides the "provisional" meaning provided by the inexact, discernible workings of providence, there must also be an "ultimate" meaning which in some way "resolves" history's residual moral obscurity (pp. 28, 102, 125, 135, 144, 214). This meaning, as we have seen, is articulated by means of such notions as the Last Judgment and the General Resurrection. According to Niebuhr, however, Christians themselves have not always understood the doctrine of "Last Things" correctly. His own account is thus closely bound up with the task of exposing what he regards as two recurring Christian errors—these being said to reflect *within* Christian thinking the mistakes of the classical and modern views, respectively.

The first error might be called "other-worldliness." It involves abandoning the hope of finding complete moral significance in the historical sphere, and seeking it beyond the course of history altogether. This may express itself in a withdrawal from the life of society or a tendency to regard it cynically—the alleged response, respectively, of the Protestant Fundamentalists and the Lutherans. The error arises from perceiving truly "the fact that the individual is always able to achieve a purer realization of meaning than can be realized communally" (pp. 198-200). The temptation is "to confine redemption to individual life." For Niebuhr, such "an individualistic and pietistic version of the Christian faith obscures the moral and social meaning of human existence and evades man's responsibility for achieving a tolerable accord with his neighbors." The second and opposite error is "this-worldliness": one to which Catholicism and Calvinism are said to be equally prone. According to Niebuhr, these seek to remedy the inexactness of historical judgments by bringing social institutions under the sovereignty of some "righteous will." For Catholics this is the Church; for Calvinists it is the rule of saints. In both instances, new evils are introduced into history by the assumption that there is, in either the Church as a redeemed community or in the saints as redeemed individuals, a "source of pure goodness and justice." In either case, "Christ ceases to be . . . a source of judgment upon the Church or the 'holy commonwealth,'" and is regarded as "its secure possession" (p. 201).

It is Niebuhr's contention that the Christian view, correctly interpreted, neither abandons hope of the "fulfillment" of history's potential moral meaning, nor concedes to any particular historic institution or state of affairs the possibility of achieving such fulfillment. It asserts that the moral obscurity we in fact find in history will somehow be made good, but it denies that this will be accomplished through further historical events. In saying this—and at the same time denying that his position is "transhistorical" in the sense of the classical theory—Niebuhr settles on difficult middle ground, the theological adequacy of which it is not our present business to question.[8] For the purpose of contrasting his approach with those of Hegel and Toynbee, however, a critical comment or two may be helpful.

It should be noted that in asserting the certainty of a "final" fulfillment of history in the way he does, Niebuhr makes a claim for revelation quite different from the one we previously examined. For the thesis that divine judgment and grace were operative (although inexactly) in history, even if said to be, in a sense, "beyond reason," was alleged to be so only in the sense of going beyond what could be *discovered* by reasoning about the course of events. In asserting, on authority of revelation, a final fulfillment which is neither wholly "beyond" history, nor something which will appear in history as a morally satisfactory state of affairs, Niebuhr asserts something "beyond reason" in a further sense: that of going "beyond rational intelligibility." As he puts it himself, the Christian revelation asserts a "mystery." The reason we have to use eschatological symbols in talking about "final" and "ultimate" meaning is that we lack—and will always lack—any clear conception of what this meaning could be. (We may well be reminded here of Hegel's general complaint about providential theories of history.)

A second comment arises out of the first. This is that Niebuhr's view, in spite of what he says about "ultimate" and "final" meanings, really denies in the end that history *itself* is fully meaningful. In spite of his attack on Christian quietism, he too is forced to look beyond history to something inexplicable and "transhistorical" for the removal of history's "moral ambiguities." There are, to be sure, occasional hints

---

[8] For theological criticism of Niebuhr, see C. W. Kegley and R. W. Bretall, eds., *Reinhold Niebuhr: His Religious, Social and Political Thought* (New York: The Macmillan Company, 1956). Available in a paperback edition.

of a different doctrine. Thus Niebuhr quotes with approval E. L. Woodward's confession: "I can indeed see evidences of design, but the pattern is on a scale beyond my comprehension" (p. 112)—seeming to leave it open that history may be fully meaningful after all, although we (by contrast with God) lack the discernment to see what its meaning is. A similar impression may be given by Niebuhr's apparent suggestion, in discussing Hebrew prophetism, that, although we find no exact "execution of a divine justice" in history, "it would be more correct to say that it does not conform to any human notion of what the divine justice should be" (p. 132). But the notion that history may be fully meaningful, in spite of its not appearing so to us, does not seem to be Niebuhr's considered view. For the most part, he seems content to say that the full meaning of history is "transhistorical," without being quite willing to say that it is "nonhistorical"—how this is possible, being left a "mystery."

The notion of "mystery" is in fact explicitly said by Niebuhr to be essential to an adequate interpretation of history. At times, indeed, it almost seems to be suggested that, for a Christian, mystery is itself a category of explanation. "The mystery of divine Providence," Niebuhr declares, "gives meaning to history" (p. 38). And again: "mystery does not annul meaning, but enriches it" (p. 103). To many critics, this is bound to look like an attempt to put the best possible face upon a difficulty. The retort might perhaps be forgiven that, as Niebuhr expounds the Christian view of history, it is that view, rather than history, which is mysterious.

For

further

reading

Carr, E. H., *What Is History?* New York: Alfred A. Knopf, Inc., 1962. A perceptive critique of historical inquiry by a historian.

Collingwood, R. G., *The Idea of History*. New York: Oxford University Press, 1946; a Galaxy book. The most considerable work on the critical side in English, in spite of having been published posthumously from papers.

Gardiner, Patrick, ed., *Theories of History*. New York: Free Press of Glencoe, Inc., 1959. Contains readings, with a good bibliography, in both speculative and critical philosophy of history. A valuable source especially for recent discussion of the problem of explanation. Expensive.

History and Theory: Studies in the Philosophy of History. A journal, published since 1961, to which both historians and philosophers contribute. An excellent bibliography, covering work done in philosophy of history between 1945 and 1957, was published in 1961.

Hook, Sidney, ed., *Philosophy and History*. New York: New York University Press, 1963. Contains papers arising out of a conference of philosophers and historians which range over the topics considered in the first half of this book. A good specimen of contemporary controversy in the field.

Löwith, Karl, *Meaning in History*. Chicago: University of Chicago Press, 1949; a Phoenix book. A stimulating discussion of the development of speculation about history.

Meyerhoff, Hans, ed., *The Philosophy of History in Our Time*. Garden City: Doubleday & Company, Inc., 1959; an Anchor book. A good anthology, especially for the problem of objectivity, drawing upon the writings of both philosophers and historians.

Walsh, W. H., *Philosophy of History: An Introduction*. New York: Harper & Row, Publishers, 1960; a Torchbook. The best general introduction. Deals with both critical and speculative questions.

INDEX

A

Achilles, 71
Alexander, Samuel, 4
Alexander the Great, 71, 74
Anaxagoras, 68
Aristotle, 60
Augustine, 60, 106-7

B

Baldwin, Stanley, 43-44, 46
Bancroft, George, 49
Barnes, Harry Elmer, 30
Barraclough, Geoffrey, 34n, 37, 64
Barzun, Jacques, 28, 43
Beale, Howard K., 47n, 50
Beard, Charles, 21-23, 27, 42, 52
Beard, Mary, 52
Becker, Carl, 22-23, 37
Beloff, Max, 38
Benson, Lee, 47n
Bergson, Henri, 85
Berlin, Isaiah, 23-26, 28, 39
Blake, Christopher, 29n, 39-40
Blyth, J. W., 91n
Bonner, T. N., 53, 54n
Brinton, Crane, 41
Brodbeck, May, 6n
Brown, John, 48
Buchanan, James, 53
Burckhardt, Jacob, 28
Butterfield, Herbert, 25, 80
114

C

Caesar, Julius, 69, 74-75
Channing, Edward, 52
Charlemagne, 73
Charles I, 8
Churchill, Winston, 42
Cicero, 75
Cohen, Jonathan, 18
Cohen, M. R., 42
Cole, A. C., 52
Collingwood, R. G., 3-4, 7-8, 10-15,
    26, 43-47, 55, 67
Comte, Auguste, 61
Condorcet, Marquis de, 62
Craven, Avery, 53
Croce, Benedetto, 3

D

Davis, Jefferson, 48, 51
Dawson, Christopher, 60
Dewey, John, 29, 31-32, 36, 39
Dilthey, Wilhelm, 3
Disraeli, Benjamin, 13, 17
Donagan, Alan, 6-7, 14-15, 17
Douglas, Stephen, 48, 53

E

Elizabeth I, 4
Engels, Friedrich, 74